HOME GYM FITNESS

FREE WEIGHT WORKOUTS

HOME GYM FITNESS
FREE WEIGHT WORKOUTS

DR. CHARLES T. KUNTZLEMAN

CB

CONTEMPORARY BOOKS

Published by Contemporary Books
An imprint of NTC/Contemporary Publishing Company
4255 West Touhy Avenue, Lincolnwood (Chicago), Illinois 60646-1975 U.S.A.
Copyright © 1985 by Charles T. Kuntzleman
Printed in the United States of America
International Standard Book Number: 0-8092-5273-2
Library of Congress Catalog Card Number: 85-7703

25   24   23   22   21   20   19   18   17   16   15   14   13   12   11   10

CONTENTS

HOME GYM FITNESS

FREE WEIGHT WORKOUTS

ACKNOWLEDGMENTS

The following companies supplied equipment and clothing for the photographs.

WEIGHT EQUIPMENT

Free Weights and Bench
Universal Gym Equipment, Inc.
PO Box 1270, Cedar Rapids, IA 52406

Heavyhands
AMF American
200 American Ave., Jefferson, IA 50129

Lace Weights
AMF-Whitely
29 Essex St., Maywood, NJ 07607

Chrome Hand Weights—Dumbbells
Diversified Products
309 Williamson Ave., PO Box 100, Opelika, AL 36802

WEIGHT CLOTHING

Shoes:

Men's Nike Challenge Court
Women's Nike Challenge Court
Nike, Inc.
3900 SW Murray Blvd., Beaverton, OR 97005

Women's Reebok Aerobic Free Style
Reebok USA, Ltd.
2933 Oceanside Blvd., Dept. NB, Oceanside, CA 92054

PREFACE

THE $16 BILLION dollar sporting goods industry is undergoing a revolution. Home fitness sales are shooting upward. In 1984, $1 billion was spent by people like you to purchase home fitness equipment. Thirty-one million Americans claimed they had exercise equipment at home.

The reasons: Costly and crowded health clubs and Americans' passion to shape up have sparked home exercise sales. People want to look good and be fit. They also want their exercise to be convenient.

It's a consumer's market, too. You can purchase literally anything in the mind-boggling arena of home exercise equipment: hand grips for $1.95 and multigyms for $19,995, bicycles for $195 or $1,995.

Thomas B. Doyle, director of information and research for the National Sporting Goods Associates, stated in 1984 that 150 manufacturers are now fighting for a piece of this hot market. Diversified Products (DP) sells 15 percent of all home exercise equipment. The next-largest companies are Huffy, AMF-Whitely, Amerec, and Vitamaster. While these are the principal companies in today's marketplace, there are also many smaller suppliers and manufacturers, and some heavy hitters have entered the field as well. The Campbell Soup Company, for example, has acquired the Triangle Manufacturing Company of Raleigh, North Carolina, a company that manufactures dumbbells. West Bend, a division of Dart Industries, bought out Total Gym in July 1983, and in April 1984 West Bend purchased PreCor, a manufacturer of treadmills, rowing machines, and exercise bicycles.

Historically, most home fitness sales have been made through chain stores—Sears, J. C. Penney, K-Mart, and Montgomery Ward. Today, many people purchase from their favorite sporting goods dealer or from a new phenomenon—a sales representative who makes house calls. No matter where or how you purchase your equipment, you'll find that these salespeople are valuable resources. They, along with the contents of this book, will show you how to get the most out of your home fitness equipment.

The most popular home equipment items are free weights, stationary bicycles and/or ergometers, and rowing machines. This book is one in a series that tells you how to get the most out of your recently purchased equipment. The series, titled *Home Gym Fitness*, includes three books that focus on the most popular pieces of equipment—stationary bicycles, rowing machines, and free weights.

In *Home Gym Fitness: Free Weight Workouts*, free weights include dumbbells, barbells, hand weights (such as HeavyHands™, ankle weights, and benches. In 1982 the U.S. Bureau of Census reported that $119.5 million was spent on weightlifting equipment. By 1983 the figure was up to $142 million, and for 1984 it was estimated that the figure will reach at least $163 million. Growth is steady.

So, read on and enjoy *Home Gym Fitness: Free Weight Workouts*. It will help you maximize the use of your free weights and help you reach new levels of fitness and exercise enjoyment.

1

THE BASICS

YOU JUST PURCHASED a set of weights. Terrific! You are now one of more than 30 million weight trainers and lifters in North America. You may feel strange, however. When you pick up a weight-training book or walk into the Y or your favorite gym, you feel intimidated by the Incredible Hulks, Amazon Women, and impressive array of equipment. You may feel out of it. Don't.

Most weight trainers and users of weights don't have incredible biceps, lats, or abs. Most don't go to gyms to work out. And most don't own extensive equipment. Look at these facts:

- According to some estimates, the average male who owns free weights is 5'10" tall and has a 38-inch chest, a 34.5-inch waist, 13.5-inch arms, 17-inch calves, and 18 percent body fat and weighs 178 pounds. The average female who owns weights is 5'4" tall and has a 34-inch chest, a 27.5-inch waist, 12-inch arms, 15.5-inch calves, and 23 percent body fat and weighs 135 pounds.
- The typical home exerciser has free weight equipment consisting of 110–150 pounds of weights plus a weight bench.
- At least 90 percent of the people who have fancy weight

machines started with free weights. They started on a small scale and gradually added to their array of equipment. They "tested the water first," however, with free weights. Sixty dollars is a lot more palatable than $600 or $6,000.

- It doesn't matter how you condition your muscles. Dr. Richard Berger, professor of physical education at Temple University, says it best: "Your muscles don't have eyes. You can overload muscles with weights, isometrics, calisthenics, or sophisticated equipment. The important thing is to overload the muscles."

FREE WEIGHTS VERSUS EXERCISE MACHINES

There are bound to be advantages and disadvantages of free weights over sophisticated machines and vice versa. First, free weights are less expensive, use less space, and can be moved easily from room to room. I take my free weights along on vacation. Second, dumbbell exercises provide opportunities to simulate certain sport skills such as swinging a baseball bat or serving a tennis ball. Third, free weights seem to be more effective in developing the smaller muscles and the stabilizer muscles of your body. Fourth, and here the research is not totally clear, many athletes report that when they switch from free weights to machines and then return to free weights, their maximum weight lifted decreases. This suggests that free weights build more strength than machines. I think the differences may be due to different techniques. So the jury is still out on that one. Fifth, since free weights allow more explosive movements than machines, more power is developed with free weights.

The first disadvantage of free weights is that it takes time to change collars and adjust weights. Therefore, the workout time with free weights is longer and less efficient than with machines. Second, free weights look messy if not properly stored. Third, with free weights, it is easy to lose your balance and leave yourself open to injury. Fourth, people using free weights tend to cheat more. That is, they use momentum or "body English" instead of strength to move the weights. Cheating reduces the effectiveness of the exercise and can increase the chances of injury. Fifth, some machines offer the ability to change resistance throughout the exercise range of motion. That is important, because the force developed in the muscles during a contraction changes as the muscle shortens. For example, when doing a curling exercise, the biceps are flexed. The weakest phase of the lift for the biceps is when the arm is completely extended. The strongest phase is when the elbow is at a 90-degree angle. The amount of the weight lifted on free weights can be no heavier than when the arm is completely extended. Machines can neutralize that difference.

The sixth disadvantage of free weights may be the most important. Most body movements, especially those used in sport, are rotary in nature. You lift barbells straight up and down. Therefore, during the basic lifts, your muscles are exercised over a relatively small range. Also, in many lifts, such as the Arm Press, the joints are locked, so the bones bear the weight and the muscles are not doing as much work as desired. Therefore, for sport, sophisticated machines may allow the rotary muscles to be developed more effectively and also tax the muscles more at the end of the exercise effort.

These are the advantages and disadvantages. It is my opinion that free weights are an acceptable, effective, and reasonably priced means for improving strength, power, muscle tone (definition), and appearance—provided, of course, that the principles outlined in this book are followed.

UNDERSTANDING FREE WEIGHT TRAINING

As beginners, you probably have many questions about the values of training with free weights. The following questions and answers should clear up any misconceptions you may have about free weights.

AM I WEIGHTLIFTING OR WEIGHT TRAINING?

Do not confuse weight training (free weights) with weightlifting or competitive bodybuilding. Weight training is the use of weights to shape, strengthen, and condition your body. Weight training can also be used to improve your strength, muscle power, and endurance for sports participation. Weightlifting, however, concentrates on specific lifts that are needed in competition or demonstration of prowess. Olympic weightlifting, for example, includes the Snatch, the Clean and Jerk, and the Press. Bodybuilding is the sport of building muscles for competitive display.

Muscles must be as fully developed as possible. The sport of bodybuilding focuses on determining whose body looks the best in terms of symmetry, form, size, and appearance. Many weightlifters and bodybuilders start with free weights.

WHAT ARE FREE WEIGHTS?

Free weights refer to dumbbells, barbells, hand weights (such as Heavyhands™), ankle weights, and benches.

WILL I BECOME MUSCLE-BOUND IF I LIFT?

A muscle-bound person is supposedly one whose muscles are so enlarged that they lack flexibility. On occasion, some weightlifters and trainers with free weights do not follow proper training principles and thus become muscle-bound. Weight training or weightlifting can firm up and strengthen your muscles without a loss of general body flexibility, provided, of course, that you lift correctly. Some massive weightlifters have great flexibility.

WILL WEIGHT TRAINING OR USING FREE WEIGHTS MAKE MEN MORE MASCULINE AND WOMEN LESS FEMININE?

The terms *masculinity* and *femininity* are subject to interpretation. Weight training will not make a female or male masculine, just as cooking will not make a male or female feminine. Masculinity and femininity are defined by genetics and attitude, not by whether or not you exercise. Traditionally, women have been told that strength and larger muscles are not ladylike. In the past, women have been encouraged to be inactive and, as a result, their figures have deteriorated.

Proper exercise, specifically training with free weights, can help to build lean body tissue. Behind every curve there is a muscle. Women who train with weights have extremely attractive figures. Women need not worry about developing huge, bulky muscles, since they do not produce enough testosterone—the hormone that helps produce larger muscles. Fortunately, in the past several years there has been a surge of interest in and acceptance of women with well-developed muscles. Rachel McLish, winner of the Ms. Olympia (1980) and 1982 Women's

World Bodybuilding Championship, says it best: "Men think I'm a dancer or some kind of athlete. They . . . never guess that I lift weights to look the way I do. Men compliment me on how great my skin looks. But it's the muscles that look good. There's no dimply fat, just muscles that are firmed and trained."

On the flip side, men (and women) sometimes equate masculinity with the size of the male's chest and biceps. Because of our culture, I would be the first to admit that an attractive male figure may be important for first impressions. But all of this is a cultural phenomenon—not a description of masculinity. Masculinity has nothing to do with size. It is a relative term. Some men are frail, yet masculine. Masculinity is in your head, not your body. It is true, however, that improved muscle development will help the male who is psychologically hung up on his physical appearance.

WHAT IS LEAN BODY TISSUE?

Lean body tissue is the muscle, bone, and organ tissue of the body. A weight-training program with free weights increases the volume of the muscle tissue. The increase in volume occurs because the muscle fibers become thicker (some have suggested that the number of fibers may increase) and because the number of mitochondria (power organism of the muscle cells) and other muscle components increases. Consequently, the muscle becomes larger and firmer. A person may gain weight, but his or her ratio of fat to muscle decreases. Weight training is the best way to increase muscle mass.

WILL MY MUSCLES TURN TO FAT IF I STOP LIFTING?

Muscles are muscles, and fat is fat. One will not change into the other. Through proper training with free weights, however, you can increase the volume of muscle in your body. The reduction of fat occurs primarily through aerobic exercise and proper eating.

It does seem as though muscle turns into fat when an athlete gives up his or her playing days. The truth is, however, that most athletes, when they stop playing their sport, continue to consume a tremendous number of calories. Unfortunately, the athlete no longer burns off as many calories because he or she is no longer physically active. Fat starts to appear. Muscles lose bulk when training is stopped. Therefore, the combination of losing muscle mass (lack of training) and increase in body fat makes it look as though the "muscle turns to fat."

AREN'T WEIGHT TRAINERS SELF-CENTERED?

Being interested in conditioning your body does not mean that you are, or will become, self-centered. Sure, mirrors are popular, and weight trainers talk about the size of their various measurements. We also have mirrors in our houses and brag about our cooking skills, business successes, intellectual powers, and marathon times.

Fitness does not improve by accident. Instead, you must deliberately work on improving your body. Weight training provides an opportunity for rapid change. When you see that your chest gets bigger, your waist smaller, your stomach flatter, and your thighs firmer, that's powerful motivation. Because weight training is intense, your muscles get a "pumped," or enlarged, firmer look after lifting for 30 minutes or so. So, fitness changes seem to appear immediately. Your muscles look bigger, stronger, and/or firmer during and after the training session. Mirrors tell you that. Therefore, lifters have an immediate payback. Mirrors provide benchmarks of improvement for free-weight exercisers.

AREN'T BIG MUSCLES USELESS MUSCLES?

That is probably a statement of envy rather than fact. Anyone who has tried training with free weights for a period of time knows that bigger muscles are stronger muscles. Stronger, more powerful muscles allow you to do things more effectively and efficiently.

CAN WEIGHT TRAINING CAUSE HIGH BLOOD PRESSURE?

Possibly. Heavy training with weights may *contribute* to higher blood pressure. J. Duncan MacDougall, Ph.D., from McMasters University in Hamilton, Ontario, showed that bodybuilders can experience dramatic increases in blood pressure when lifting. MacDougall tested the blood pressure of five experienced bodybuilders, aged 22–28, who did *heavy lifting*. A series of Double-Leg Presses produced an average blood pressure of 355/281 mm HG in one person. An average blood pressure of 295/230 mm Hg was shown after a series of Single-Arm Curls. The high side of a normal resting blood pressure is 140/90 mm Hg. I think the elevated blood pressure in some weight trainers may be due to their diet, improper lifting, excessive training, body weight, and obsessive-compulsive personalities. To reduce the chance of elevated blood pressure, follow the principles outlined in this book.

ISN'T IT TRUE THAT WEIGHT TRAINING IS FOR YOUNG PEOPLE ONLY?

Healthy people of any age can lift weights. Many older people work out regularly with weights. Some dramatic results can be achieved by middle-aged free weight exercisers.

WHAT IS THE DIFFERENCE BETWEEN BODY SCULPTING AND BODYBUILDING?

Because of the interest in women's weight training, the terms *bodybuilding* and *body sculpting* have presented some confusion. *Shape* magazine calls it "mass" versus "class."

Bodybuilding is the building of muscle mass. It applies to men and women. Bigger is better as long as there is symmetry in the build. That is, the upper body must be proportionate to the lower body is size and form.

Body sculpting is the development of a more aesthetic classical look, that is, the development of a more traditional feminine muscular structure.

The "mass versus class" controversy is probably one of physiology. Some women will build more "mass" because they produce more testosterone or take steroids. Others, because of a more typical makeup and genetic predisposition, develop less bulk, more "traditional" lines—class.

2

THE BENEFITS

THERE ARE MANY benefits of training with free weights. The degree to which you will achieve these benefits depends on your dedication, genetic predisposition and/or body type, and training techniques.

Your dedication is evidenced by the number of minutes you train, the number of exercises you do in each session, and the number of times you train each week. For example, if you exercise 45-60 minutes three times a week, the changes will come quickly. Also, the benefits will be heightened if you do the lifts correctly.

Your genetic predisposition (body type) also dictates your rate of improvement:

1. If there's a tendency in your family toward obesity (your mother and father were or are fat), you can conclude that you, too, will (or do) possess a roundness or softness. If not now, then in the future (at middle age), you will tend to put on fat. This type of person is called an *endomorph*.

2. If at one time your parents had good physiques, but as they aged things seemed to go to pot (with males, the proverbial beer belly), you probably possess a good physique. If not now, then in the past, you cut a nice figure. This type of person is called a *mesomorph*.

3. If there is a natural tendency toward thinness in your family, you will probably remain this way throughout your life. You are called an *ectomorph*.

There are exceptions to these rules, but the above categories probably apply to about 75 percent of the population. Therefore, expect the following progress with free weights:

Endomorphs: Your progess with free weights will probably be slower than for most people. Even then, you still may not get an "ideal" shape. Your body will have a softer appearance—you will not look sinewy. Keep the faith, however. Progress will be made, and your body will look a lot better.

Mesomorphs: Your progress with free weights will be rapid. Dedication can help you develop an "ideal" shape. You will rapidly improve your lean body tissue. Muscle definition will be striking.

Ectomorphs: Your progress with free weights will be average, and progress will be more rapid than for mesomorphs. Training with free weights will not produce an "ideal" shape, but muscle definition will be improved substantially. Your body should fill out where for years it has been overly thin.

Finally, the training techniques outlined in Chapter 5 will allow you to tailor-make the program for your own needs.

With these limitations in mind, here are the benefits you can expect to achieve by training with free weights.

A BETTER-LOOKING BODY

One of the greatest advantages of a free weight training program is that, properly designed, it will provide you with a better-looking, better-proportioned, and stronger body. We all know what happens to our bodies when we don't exercise. Those nearly perfect, youthful bodies that we had during our teenage years begin to develop fat where it's unwanted. Sags and bulges appear. Conversely, we become thin where at one time we were well formed. Our waist expands while our chest decreases. Many women find themselves with sagging breasts and cottage-cheese thighs. Both men and women find that they start to slouch, waddle, and feel as though they are teetering off-balance. The reason: their weight is in all the wrong places.

Fortunately, these things can be remedied. One of the best ways is with a specific free weight training program that concentrates on specific body parts. I'm not suggesting that fat is removed from one area of the body (spot reducing). Instead, the firmness of the muscles is improved and lean body tissue increased. In short, your body looks better.

POSTURE

Training with free weights improves your posture. Watch the way people sit. Some are slumpers; others are fit and trim and sit well. When they get up to walk, there is diversity again. Some are slouching, and at the other extreme are people who seem to maintain an excellent pose.

Good posture does not come naturally to most of us. We have to work at it. Some of us may have had good posture when we were young, but we lost it as we grew older. The loss of good posture is due to lack of muscle fitness or osteoporosis. *Osteoporosis* is a bone demineralization caused by poor nutrition (lack of calcium) and inadequate exercise in women. The result is deteriorating posture (slouched shoulders). Once the antigravity muscles (those that help you stand, walk, and sit properly) are trained, you'll place less strain on these muscles, ending up with fewer back problems and suffering less fatigue. To help combat osteoporosis, exercise is important. Exercises for the upper back and higher calcium intake go a long way toward preventing or slowing osteoporosis. Better posture makes you more attractive. It also helps you give a better impression.

BETTER WEIGHT CONTROL

Weight control is a strange and emotional issue in American society. People tend to talk in terms of pounds when they think about weight. In this book, I refer to shape and symmetry. Unfortunately, weight has little to do with how you look. Many people may be 5'3" and weigh 115 pounds (right on, according to the height-weight charts), yet when you look at them in a bathing suit, you notice that they are soft and flabby. Conversely, there is the professional football player who is 6'2" and weighs 235 pounds. That person is well overweight according to the height-weight charts, but his body looks good. His waist may be 32 inches and his chest 45 inches. His body is well muscled and attractive.

With both the male and female, think in terms of lean body tissue and fat—not weight. The goal is to keep body fat low and lean body tissue high. One of the best ways to build lean body tissue is through free weight training. Working on muscles such as the arms, legs, abdomen, and chest will build lean body tissue by increasing the muscle fiber size and the strength of the muscle. Consequently, the muscles become denser and heavier. As a result, you may weigh more, according to the scale, than you did before. However, your body may look better because the chest is larger in comparison to the waist. Your dress size is smaller, or you've just pulled your belt one notch tighter. People usually say, "I didn't lose weight; I simply rearranged it."

Training with free weights and the building of lean body tissue play another interesting role in fat control. A person with well-conditioned muscles burns off more calories for any given activity than a person who carries more body fat. The reason for this phenomenon is that muscles demand more oxygen than fat. If there is more muscle in the body, it stands to reason, then, that more oxygen is consumed. Oxygen consumption and calorie expenditure mean the same thing. Therefore, an increase in oxygen consumption means an increase in calories used.

Training with free weights may also aid in weight control by decreasing your appetite. If you do your weight-training exercises shortly before mealtime, you may find yourself eating less at that meal. The reason is still a subject for a great deal of speculation. Researchers suggest that the reason for the decreased appetite may be the result of physiological, psychological, and cultural determinants. Physiologically, you may want to eat less after a workout because the blood flow of your body is diverted from the stomach to the exercised muscles. Also, an increase in body temperature depresses appetite. Psychologically, you may eat less now. Regular exercise has taught you that you control more than one part of your life. Once exercise is under control, you then proceed to get your eating under control. Also, you may eat less because instead of watching TV, downing soda pop and chips, you are pumping iron.

IMPROVED MENTAL ATTITUDE

People who have been on a free weight training program for a period of time note that they feel great. They feel great because they have a better-looking body, better posture, and better muscle-to-fat ratio. But it goes beyond that.

While I won't go into *all* the details, an impressive array of researchers have noted that regular vigorous exercise can contribute to an improved mental attitude through a reduction in neuromuscular headaches, anger, anxiety, and depression. It may also improve creativity, self-esteem, and mental outlook.

Neuromuscular Headaches. Dr. Herbert deVries of the Gerontology Center at the University of California showed that men 50 years or older had a reduction in headaches with increased physical activity—without medication.

Anger and Anxiety. Dr. William Morgan at the University of Wisconsin reported that after a vigorous workout there was a measurable decrease in anxiety. The level of adrenaline in the blood, the blood pressure, and the heart rate were reduced. Clinically, many people report improved moods and less anxiety after a good bout of strenuous exercise. Many experts call exercise the world's best tranquilizer.

Depression and Blues. Studies at the University of Virginia suggest that vigorous exercise—aerobic or non-aerobic— can be a mood elevator. This mood elevation may come from a secretion of beta endorphins (so-called "mood elevators") by the brain. The mood elevation may also come from a sense of accomplishment, purpose, or control in one area of your life.

Creativity. A change of scenery may go a long way in helping you utilize your creativity to its fullest. The late Dr. Hans Selye said it best: "Stress on one system helps to relax another." In other words, you may be struggling with a thorny occupational, domestic, or personal problem. The struggle is emotionally overwhelming. If you temporarily leave the problem and exercise—with free weights, for example—you relax your emotional being and exhaust your physical being. After a good 30- to 60-minute workout, you may be charged up and ready to tackle the unresolved problem.

Confidence. Good fitness builds confidence. Dr. T. K. Cureton, the grandfather of fitness in the U.S., conducted research at the University of Illinois for more than three decades. His exhaustive work convinced him that most middle-aged men lose confidence in their physical ability as they get older. They become unfit, have sagging waistlines and flabby chests and arms. Since men are taught early in life that manliness and physical vigor go hand in hand, their self-confidence slips. When self-confidence slips, the mental and emotional areas of their lives are affected as well. Exercise, such as free weight training, can turn this around. When muscles firm up, stomachs flatten, and chests expand, confidence may increase.

Men are not the only ones affected. Stacey Bentley, who entered the Zane Invitational (bodybuilding) in 1980 and defeated the legendary Rachel McLish and many other top bodybuilding professionals, recalls: "I was a fat and insecure teenage girl. I weighed 140 pounds at one point and was totally afraid to assert myself. Bodybuilding completely changed my life, believe me."

Need I say more?

ADDED HEALTH BENEFITS

Most people go through life suffering annoying aches and pains. Most of us assume that these ailments are the result of getting older. Surprisingly, these troublesome pains often disappear when you work at doing specific muscle-training exercises. Sixty percent of your body weight is muscle. Usually the first sign of tension appears in the largest organ of your body—your muscles. Basically, your muscles are crying for activity. When you exercise muscles regularly and deliberately, you effectively reduce tension that may be occurring because of a buildup of excessive hormones and nervous tension.

Another benefit of free weight training is the potential for alleviation of varicose veins. Obese and unconditioned people (usually those with large abdomens) and pregnant women are especially susceptible to varicose veins. The protruding abdomen allows the abdominal organs to slip downward and forward. As a result, abdominal pressure is exerted on the large veins in the legs. This pressure, in turn, restricts the blood flow and causes the valves in the veins to function improperly. As a result, blood can pool and push the veins toward the body surface, causing the unsightly condition we often call *varicose veins*.

Strengthening the abdominal muscles will help hold the abdominal organs in place and thus alleviate or prevent pressure on the leg veins. In addition, training with free weights for the legs will strengthen your leg muscles and contribute to holding the veins in their proper place.

Training with free weights is not a panacea for all your aches, ailments, and figure faults. But free weights make a contribution to your physical and mental well-being. A regular program of free weight training can make your body look better, feel better, and be stronger. The proper weight-training program can fashion your body into one you can be proud of and can provide substantial appearance, strength, health, and sport benefits.

IMPROVING PHYSICAL FITNESS ELEMENTS

Training with free weights helps you improve essentials of physical fitness. In fact, muscle fitness is usually improved more effectively through free weight training than through any other type of exercise.

Muscle fitness has three components—strength, endurance, and power. Muscular strength is the ability of a muscle or group of muscles to exert a maximum force in a single exertion, for example, the number of pounds you can lift from the floor at one time. Muscle endurance is the ability of a muscle or group of muscles to repeat movements over and over or to hold a particular position for a long period of time, for example, the number of times you can curl a relatively light weight. A third area of muscle fitness is power. This component has more to do with sport success than with health or fitness. Power is a combination of strength and speed, that is, the ability to lift or move a weight quickly. Good examples include the high jump, standing long jump, and tennis serve.

Usually an improvement in muscle strength, endurance, or power also improves the appearance and definition of your muscles.

BUILDING MUSCLE STRENGTH

Muscle strength is improved through systematic training of the muscles. Training with free weights is one of the easiest and most economical ways to improve your muscular strength. You have probably heard the story of the person who was an active runner and could run a 10K in 35 minutes or less. He bragged about his great physical shape. One day his wife, a devoted gardener, asked him to help transplant some bushes. The runner quickly discovered that he was unable to lift the bushes without hurting his back. The necessary effort far exceeded his expectations. Then there was the woman who could break three hours in the marathon but failed the National Fitness Test because she did not do well on the push-up or sit-up tests. Both these illustrations demonstrate that these people did not have the muscular strength to perform the tasks that appeared so simple. While they could run and demonstrate great cardiovascular fitness, they did not have much strength.

Clearly, muscle strength is important to overall good health and to getting you through the day. For example, if you have inadequate muscle strength, when you get up in the morning you won't be able to assume a correct posture. You will also be unable to do certain tasks or handle emergencies such as lifting a heavy suitcase out of the trunk, pushing the car when it is stuck in the mud, shoveling snow, or lifting bushes. It has also been shown that people with poor muscle strength tend to have poor posture, which can set them up for low-back pain or other injuries.

MUSCLE ENDURANCE

Closely allied to muscular strength is muscle endurance. There is an interesting relationship between these two. You must have adequate muscle strength to hold yourself in a correct posture or to lift the suitcase out of the trunk. But you need good muscle endurance so you can hold yourself in a correct posture all day or carry your suitcase from the trunk of your car to the ticket counter of the airport.

It is surprising how many kinds of ordinary activities require muscle endurance. Concert piano playing requires it. The bricklayer who works all day has good muscle endurance for that activity. The long-distance bicycle rider or cross-country skier needs this quality and plenty of it. The person working around the house or in the garden benefits from better muscle endurance. As you can see, the common thread that runs through all these activities is the extended effort required.

You probably know people who can put forth an amazing burst of strength for an instant but have no staying power. In other words, they can pull themselves up only one time. That's strength. On the other hand, there are people who can do 15 pull-ups. That's strength combined with muscle endurance.

INCREASING PHYSICAL POWER

Power is a combination of strength and speed. It is super to be able to perform the task that a strong person can perform, but it is not very helpful in sport if you move slowly. Athletics often call for both strength and quick movement. Playing tennis is a good example. Sprinting and playing football or basketball are others. Power may not directly affect your health and well-being, but it certainly has important implications for participation in sport. The person with power is usually the victor in sports.

AEROBIC CAPACITY

You can improve your aerobic fitness with free weights. The primary method to improve aerobic capacity involves moving rapidly from exercise to exercise and keeping the heart rate elevated throughout the workout (more on this later). This technique is called *aerobic weight training* or *circuit training*. The results you get from aerobic weight training won't be as impressive as what you get from running, bicycling, or swimming, but improvements do occur. For example, running improves aerobic capacity by about 20–30 percent; training with free weights through circuit training improves aerobic capacity by up to 7 percent.

3

WHAT SHOULD YOU EXPECT?

TRAINING WITH FREE weights means systematically training the various muscles of your body with hand-held weights or with weights attached to the legs. This training improves the appearance and firmness of your body. It also improves your muscle strength, muscle endurance, and/or muscle size. Before beginning any program, it is important to understand eight key principles of training.

1. INDIVIDUAL RATES OF RESPONSE

The first and most important principle is the *individual rate of response*. Each person has his own rate of response to a training program. It seems as though some people can arrive at a high level of physical condition long before others. The reasons for this difference are not clear, but there probably are several of them.

AGE

Age is one factor. Obviously, the younger you are, the greater your rate of improvement. The longer you have been deteriorating, the longer it has been since you've been involved in fitness programs, the harder it is to come back. The older you are, the slower the regenerative powers of the body. That doesn't mean it is impossible; it just means that it may take more time. Therefore, the older you are, the more patient you will need to be. The changes will be slower in coming.

PHYSICAL CONDITION

A second factor, many times closely allied to age, is your physical condition. While some people who are 40 years of age are in better shape than 20-year-olds, it seems that age and physical condition go together. Many times, a 40-year-old decides to get back in shape and hasn't done anything for 20 years, while a 20-year-old who makes a commitment to exercise may have been out of shape for one year.

If your physical condition is poor, the improvement will be slower in coming, and you will not be able to tolerate a work load of much intensity during the first few weeks or even months. Because fitness levels are so low, however, tremendous improvements may be expected—in some instances improvement of 100 percent or more. On the flip side of the coin, it is also true that if you are in excellent physical condition to start with you may be able to tolerate heavy work loads, but your improvement may be restricted to the 5- to 10-percent range.

BODY TYPE

As mentioned in the previous chapter, your body type plays a role in your rate of improvement. If you are the type of person who at one time was muscular, you will see rapid improvements as a result of a training program. If you are a thin person such as a long-distance runner type, you may find that you will never really develop large muscles like those of a bulky football player, although you *will* improve. If you have a tendency toward obesity, you may also find that changes that occur do so much more slowly simply because you carry a great deal of body fat.

SLEEP AND REST HABITS

In addition to age, physical condition, and body type, your rest, sleep, and relaxation are important factors in the progress you make. For example, if you aren't getting adequate rest, sleep, or relaxation, you may find that all the exercise is causing you literally to "burn the candle at both ends." If you are going to train, you must also provide adequate rest and relaxation. This is particularly true once you are past the age of 30. Although the same could be said for those under 30, it becomes much more obvious once you reach so-called "middle age."

FOOD AND NUTRITION

The quality of the food you put into your body will also play a role in your individual rate of response. If you are training hard but not fueling your body appropriately, and you're getting the wrong kinds of food (particularly foods high in sugar, fat, and sodium), you are not going to see nearly the change you would if you ate a more balanced diet. An appropriate eating regimen is the U.S. Dietary Guidelines, which recommend a diet made up of the following components:

- 58 percent carbohydrate: 48 percent complex carbohydrate in the form of grains and vegetables; and 10 percent simple sugar such as honey, table sugar, and corn syrup
- 12 percent protein: dairy products, eggs, meat and meat products, some vegetables and grains
- 30 percent fat: egg yolks, oils, creams, butter, etc.

This type of diet is better than one based on convenience foods such as fast-food restaurant fare, packaged and canned foods.

INJURIES

If you seem to be plagued by injuries more frequently than other people, your rate of response is not going to be nearly as fast. If you have chronic joint problems, various aches and pains, your training will be restricted, so your rate of improvement will not be as fast as low-injury people.

MOTIVATION

Last, but certainly not least, is your basic motivation. Some people are simply better motivated than others. They exercise three or four times a week as recommended. Other are much more sporadic. Dedication and motivation are important to your rate of response in training with free weights.

2. SKILL

Closely allied to your individual rate of response is your skill level. You may attribute much of your improvement during the early stages of training with weights to improvements in muscle strength. The real reason, however, is an improvement in your lifting skills, in learning how to do the exercise correctly. For example, the first time you try to bench press a weight, you might be able to press no more than 60 pounds, but at the end of the week you are able to do 80 pounds. The improvement is due not to increased strength, but to improved technique. Competitive lifters capitalize on skill importance and spend a good bit of time improving their techniques so they can lift much heavier weights.

As with everything in life, people differ greatly in their ability to learn new skills. Some people are physically gifted. They learn a new skill quickly. Therefore, they make quick progress and are able to lift more than the average person during the first few weeks of training.

3. USE AND DISUSE

Another principle that must be considered is the "use and disuse" principle. Simply, it means "use it or lose it." If you require a part of your body to perform a certain task, the efficiency of that part will remain the same or improve. On the other hand, if you do not require a certain part of your body to perform a selected task, the efficiency of that part will degenerate. Muscles grow larger and stronger when exercised. Underexercised muscles decrease. Use promotes function.

Understanding these three principles makes it easier to apply the next five.

4. OVERLOAD

The overload principle is the basic tenet in training, especially a free weight training program. Overloading means that when your muscles are repeatedly and regularly stimulated by a greater-than-normal weight and number of exercises, your muscles adjust and increase their capacity to perform physical work. If you want to improve your strength, your muscles must repeatedly be subjected to a training routine that stresses the muscles more than normal. As soon as your body becomes accustomed to that exercise—that is, as soon as you no longer feel the exercise is demanding—you must increase the work (overload) so that your body is stimulated by the greater-than-normal exercise load.

There are many ways to overload. One way is to increase the weight, which is usually done to improve strength. A second way is to increase the duration of the exercise, that is, the number of seconds you do a particular exercise. An increase in duration results in an improvement of muscle endurance. The third method of overload, which is implied in the second, involves increasing the number of repetitions of the exercise. This, too, improves muscle endurance. The fourth technique is to increase both the weight and the length of time (strength and endurance). A fifth method might be to decrease the rest period between lifts (strength or endurance). A sixth is to increase the speed of movement (power).

5. ADAPTATION

When your muscles are repeatedly exercised and overloaded, they eventually adapt over the weeks or months to the overload. If the body is made to work harder, it will soon be able to work harder. Generally, adaptation is measured by the improvement in performance, a principle that is important in establishing an exercise program. Athletes know this explicitly. Out of shape at the start of the season, they train for weeks to condition and harden their bodies. Their muscles adapt, and they get into shape. For example, suppose you are currently engaged in a free weight training program that involves curling 35 pounds 10 times. At first the schedule may be demanding (overload), leaving you exhausted. After a period of weeks you will find that the lift becomes easier and less fatiguing (adaptation). In fact, lifting 45 pounds 10 times soon becomes quite easy. Your body has adapted to the exercise work load imposed on it.

6. PROGRESSION

Just the fact that your body has adapted to a certain overload does not mean you should add 25 pounds to overload the muscles and wait for them to adapt. Instead, a gradual approach of adding from 2½ to 5 pounds is more appropriate. The gradual approach to overloading and adapting is called *progression*. When you begin lifting, you are able to curl 35 pounds 10 times each day. Soon that level is no longer demanding to your body. You have adapted. You are no longer overloading your muscles. Now you must progressively increase the weight by lifting 40 pounds 10 times. You have overloaded the muscles again. An alternative approach would be to lift the 35 pounds 15 times.

Note that, in each instance, the increases were rather small. They were what weight-training experts call *progressive*. This means that the increments were significant enough to present a new challenge to your body but not enough to leave you completely exhausted.

Progression enables you to increase your work load gradually. Muscles usually do not become sore, and the likelihood of overtaxing or even injuring the body during the training will be reduced. Failure to increase in a progressive manner can lead only to frustration and pain.

7. SPECIFICITY

Specificity means that improvements made in training are related directly to the type of training followed. For example, if you follow a strength-training program with free weights, you will not improve muscle endurance. Similarly, a flexibility program like yoga does little to improve strength or endurance.

Many athletes have experienced this phenomenon of specificity. Swimmers serve as a good example. Swimmers may consider themselves to be in great condition until they find, when attempting to play a vigorous game of basketball, that they are forced to slow down and pace themselves. The reason for the apparent lack of conditioning for basketball is due to the principle of specificity.

Working one area of the body will not improve another. If you spend all your time developing your upper body with weights, for example, the muscles of your lower body will not benefit.

You must work most of the major muscle groups of your body if you expect to develop total muscle fitness. You can't work on just the legs and expect your upper body to improve, or vice versa. Most important, you must understand that training with free weights does not condition or strengthen the heart and lungs, important keys to true physical fitness. The only way that weight training can do this is if you engage in aerobic weight training, which will help improve your aerobic capacity about 5–7 percent.

8. RETROGRESSION

The last principle of training with free weights is retrogression. You will occasionally find that your performance seems to be off the usual pace. Try as you might, you cannot curl 35 pounds 10 times, even though you may have done this for the past three weeks. The reason for this decline or fall in performance is called *retrogression*. Experts really don't know the basic cause. The decline probably has something to do with the ability of the body to mobilize its resources for meeting the overload imposed on it. When the body adjusts, you then begin to reach your typical level of performance.

On occasion, retrogression is a result of poor diet, inadequate sleep or rest, lack of motivation, and/or improper conditioning or training. Regardless of the cause, it is important that you constantly elevate your current condition. Be sure that your nutrition is good, your rest and sleep are sufficient, and your training techniques are proper. If you retrogress by more than 10 percent in performance in a week, you may try reducing the overload for a few days or switch to another activity. After the appraisal and tapering off, improvement is bound to follow. Don't be discouraged. Retrogression is common, though frustrating.

The eight basic principles of training are to be remembered when training with free weights. The principles will not only help you maximize your fitness potential; they will also help you understand why and how these changes take place.

It is important that you lift a weighted bar from the floor correctly. Stand close to the bar so that when you reach down to grip the bar your shins almost touch the bar. Your feet should be hip-width apart. Your hands should be shoulder-width apart and palms facing backward (overhand grip). Grip the bar firmly and lower your hips and raise your head slightly, as illustrated. *Your hips should be lower than your shoulders.* As you lift the power should come from your legs—by straightening them. Do NOT lift with your back.

4

GETTING STARTED

TRAINING WITH FREE weights is a relatively safe sport. In fact, of all reported injuries in sports, only 1 percent is related to weightlifting and weight training. Two-thirds of these injuries are minor and need no emergency treatment.

SAFETY

Despite this safety record, training with free weights can be made safer:

1. You must *learn the proper techniques for performing the various exercises.*

2. Before lifting, make sure the equipment is in proper working order. If your free weights have collars, be certain they are in good working order and are secured tightly to the bar.

3. Listen to your body. If you proceed too fast and attempt to lift too much too soon, your body will let you know. It will "talk" to you. So listen. Here are some ways your body will tell you that you're overdoing:

- breathlessness (excessive)
- chest pain
- dizziness or light-headedness
- nausea
- persistent joint or muscle pain
- throbbing head

27

Before lifting, collars should be securely tightened.

4. Breathe properly.

- Inhale as you lift the weight; exhale when lowering.
- Do not hold your breath when lifting light weights—breathe normally.
- Hold your breath *briefly* at the hardest part of lifting a heavy weight.
- *Exhale* forcefully as you pass the brief breath-holding phase of the heavy lift. This exhalation relieves the pressure in the chest.

5. Don't lift with your back. Some people "put their back into it" when lifting, particularly while lifting a weight off the floor. Lift with your legs.

6. Lift with a partner. This is especially important if the weights are heavy.

7. Move the weight through the full range of motion. You will cheat yourself if you don't put the muscle or muscle group through the full range of motion. For example, if you are doing the Curl exercise, you will want to start the exercise with the arms fully extended and finish with the arms drawn as close to the chest as possible. By doing the exercise in this manner, you will not lose

Be certain you extend and contract your muscles as far as possible.

Do not use muscle substitutions when exercising. If you must cheat to get the weight to the correct position, the weight is too heavy.

flexibility, since both the biceps (muscle on the front of the upper arms) and triceps (muscle on the back of the upper arms) are completely extended and contracted.

8. Don't cheat. There is a natural tendency to use "body English" or muscle substitutions to lift a heavy weight or to finish the prescribed number of repetitions. Don't fall into this trap. *Cheating*, as it is called in weight-training parlance, reduces the effectiveness of the exercise and on rare occasions may injure you.

9. Do the exercises as described. These exercises were selected because of their effectiveness and relative safety. To maximize their safety, do not modify the exercises because "that's the way I did it before." Recent research has shown certain exercises to be harmful to particular parts of the body—particularly the knee and low back.

EQUIPMENT

BARBELLS AND DUMBBELLS

The barbell is usually four feet to seven feet long. The bar itself is about an inch in diameter. Many barbells have a sleeve that fits and revolves around the bar. Inside collars separate the weights from the sleeve and outside collars hold the weight plates in place.

Your home barbell set is probably 110 pounds in weight. Usually 90–95 pounds of the set are plates. The remaining 15–20 pounds are bars, collars, and sleeves. The bar alone in the photo weighs 45 pounds.

Bars with special configurations for special lifts—e.g., a curling bar for a Biceps Curl—are available.

The dumbbell is really a very short barbell, 12–18 inches in length. It has inside and outside rollers to hold the weight plates. The weight plates are made of the same substance as the barbell plates. Sleeves are also usually present. At the present time, many dumbbells have a fixed poundage. Fixed-weight dumbbells may range from 1 to 75 pounds or more. Most fixed-weight dumbbells for the home market weigh 1–20 pounds. These fixed-weight dumbbells are more attractive than the adjustable kind. Unfortunately, you must purchase several sets of different weights because you will need to add weight progressively to build strength and power. Some of the newer, so-called "solid-piece" weights do provide for adding weight in the form of sand, pellets, and weight bars.

As you would expect, there are many variations of the above. There are chrome-plated—even gold-plated!—plates and bars.

Plates. Weight plates, interchangeable for barbells and dumbbells, are available in either coated or uncoated iron or in vinyl-covered sand, pellets, or concrete. Cast-iron weights are stronger and more expensive, while the vinyl-covered plates are quieter but a bit more fragile.

Collars. Collars are the devices on the barbell or dumbbell that hold the weight plates in place. Inside collars separate the weights from the sleeve or keep the plates from sliding inward. Outside collars keep the plates from moving off the end of the bar. With some sets, the collars are locked in place with a wrench. Others have a variety of locking devices built into the collars.

Barbell and dumbbell set.

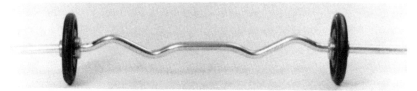

The curling bar.

Adjustable dumbbells, fixed-weight dumbbells, and chrome adjustable dumbbells

Collars may come in different shapes and sizes.

WRIST AND ANKLE WEIGHTS

Numerous companies manufacture wrist and ankle weights. These come in one- to five-pound (or more) sizes with Velcro® Lock Fasteners for secure attachment to the body. The weights are worn by exercisers while running, walking, and exercising in general. As an alternative, some exercisers even carry one- to five-pound dumbbells when running or doing selected exercises.

Some ankle and wrist weights, such as AMF-Whitely, are adjustable. The nylon casings of the wrist and ankle weights have pouches that allow insertion of cylindrical lead weights of one-half pound each. A more recent modification of the ankle weights are lace weights by AMF. These are little pouches that are laced on the shoe. The pouches then hold weights of various sizes. Men usually wear these weights to overload the limbs being exercised—legs, arms, possibly shoulders—that is, to condition, strengthen, tone, and increase the size of the muscles. Women, on the other hand, usually wear these weights to increase the energy expenditure of an activity—running, dancing, and walking. With wrist and ankle weights, you burn more calories and therefore supposedly lose weight and decrease girth measurements.

If you wear these weights when running, dancing, etc., you may use up to 30 percent more calories. Therefore, a run of three miles that might normally use up to 300 calories might burn 390 calories with wrist or ankle weights. If you do that every day for a year, that amounts to an extra nine pounds of *fat* lost each year!

All this means that these weights will help you reshape your body to become more attractive. Certain girths, such as the calves, might consequentially become larger, but then some girths, such as ankles, may get smaller. Your legs will be better-looking. Also, while you will increase muscle mass, you will decrease body fat. The changes may not be apparent on the scale, but they will be obvious in the mirror.

Heavyhands™. Recently, there has been a significant adaptation of the wrist weights concept. Leonard Schwartz, M.D., a physician from Pittsburgh, Pennsylvania, has devised a method of carrying specialized weights in the hands. Called Heavyhands™, it has caused a mild revolution among some exercisers. The trademarked Heavyhands is nothing more than weights that include a strap or bar that cradles the hand. Both the shaft and strap are covered with soft rubber. The design allows you to be

Wrist weights with Velcro® strap.

Lace weights are laced onto your running shoes.

Heavyhands™.

less consciously concerned about hanging on to the weights.

Iron Boots. Instead of the weights, you can use iron boots, which are not actually boots at all. Instead, they are metal bases (large soles) that can be attached to your shoes with straps. They have center holes through which metal bars are inserted and to which the weight plates are attached to bring the weight up to the desired poundage.

BENCHES

Good lifting benches consist of metal framing and padding of some type. They are usually 10-14 inches wide, about 18 inches high, and 3-5 feet in length. A bench is a must to get the most from your free weight workout. The best bench includes a metal holder to support the barbell before and after bench pressing. For added versatility, many of the good benches are adjustable in the back and leg areas. Many have leg curl machines to work the lower part of the body. At first, you may be satisfied with only barbells and dumbbells.

The bench is useful for chest exercises because it allows the shoulders and arms to hang below the level of the chest, thus permitting the pectoralis, the major muscles of the upper chest, to be worked from a lengthened position.

If you are serious, it's only a matter of time before you'll find that a bench which allows for leg development and adjustable incline is mandatory.

INCLINE BOARDS

Many of the chest and abdominal exercises are performed from an incline board or bench. An incline board allows you to overload the abdominal muscles more effectively. By placing the board in an incline position, you mount the board with the head lower than the legs. From this position, you must overcome gravity to do various sit-up exercises.

A weight bench with rack allows you to do bench presses safely.

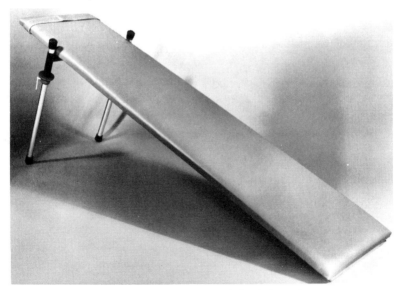

An incline board can be used to overload your abdominal muscles.

EXERCISE TERMS

Body Tone or Toning. This term is often used incorrectly. Here it means the conditioning, shaping, and strengthening of the body through free-weight training.

Grips. You can grasp the bar in three different ways:

- *Overhand Grip:* Your hands grip the bar so that your palms face toward the legs and thumbs are toward each other (see photo).
- *Underhand Grip:* This grip is the opposite of the overhead grip in that the palms face away from the legs as the bar is gripped (see photo).
- *Alternate Grip:* Here, one hand takes an overhand grip and the other an underhand grip (see photo).

Range of Motion. This is the distance through which a ligament can be turned at a particular joint.

Repetitions (Reps and Sets). *Reps* are the number of times you do a particular exercise; for example, 6, 8, or 10 times. *Sets* are the number of groups of repetitions for a particular exercise, such as three sets of eight repetitions of Barbell Curls. That means you do eight repetitions of Barbell Curls three times.

Resistance. This is the weight moved by a muscular contraction.

Valsalva Phenomenon. This is associated with holding your breath during heavy lifting. If the throat is kept closed during a heavy lift, the pressure in the chest increases and prevents the blood from returning to the heart. At first, blood pressure increases, but if the exertion is extended, the chest pressure increases. Then blood pressure falls quickly because of the decreased blood flow to the heart. Therefore, it is *essential* that you breathe correctly (as explained earlier in this chapter).

Overhand Grip.

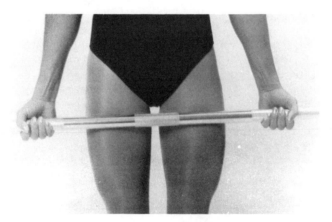

Underhand Grip.

Alternate Grip.

BODY PARTS

Throughout this book, you will read a great many terms used to describe body parts and muscles. To familiarize yourself with muscle terminology, the table below may help.

BODY PART	SLANG	NAME OF MUSCLES
Upper Third		
Neck (back of)	Traps	Trapezius
(front of)	—	Sternocleidomastoid
Shoulders (next to neck)	Traps	Trapezius
(farther away)	Delts	Deltoids
Upper Back (high)	Traps	Trapezius
(middle)	Lats	Latissimus Dorsi
Upper Arms (front)	Bis	Biceps
(back)	Tris	Triceps
Forearms (front)	Flexors	Flexor Group
(back)	Extensors	Extensor Group
Chest (front of chest)	Pecs	Pectoralis Major
(side of chest)	—	Serratus Anterior
Middle Third		
Stomach/Abdomen	Abs	Rectus Abdominus
Waist	Obliques	External & Internal Obliques
Hips	Hip	Gluteus Medius Tensor Fascia Latae
Buttocks	Glutes	Gluteus Maximus
Outer Thighs	Saddle Bags	Tenso Fascia Latae Gluteus Maximus Iliotibial Tract
Low Back	Back	Erector Spinae
Lower Third		
Thighs (inside)	Inner Thigh	Hip Adductors
(front)	Quads	Quadriceps Femoris
(back)	Hamstrings (Hams)	Biceps Femoris Semitendinosus Semimembranosus
Calves (front)	Shins	Tibialis Anterior
(back)	Gastroc	Gastrocnemius

You should also know the two terms below.

Cartilage. Cartilage is the tough, fibrous tissue that forms a cushion between bones and protects them from shock.

Ligament. Ligaments are tissues that fasten bones together and hold organs in place. Ligaments may appear as cords, bands, or sheets. A sprain occurs when ligaments covering a joint are twisted or torn.

5

THE WORKOUT PROGRAMS

BEFORE YOU BEGIN an exercise free weight program, you must ask yourself the question: What do I want to get out of my program? Once you have answered that question, you will know where to begin and what type of program is best for you.

In this chapter there are four plans, each based on a different goal but all involving exercising with free weights.

The first is intended to improve muscle endurance and/or body toning and appearance. Here, lean body tissue will be increased and your muscles will appear better formed and conditioned. The muscles will not become bulky in size. Plan 2 involves exercising for strength or "bulking up." This is a technique many bodybuilders use to develop massive physiques. Plan 3 is exercising for power, sport, and bodybuilding. Athletes should use this technique to prepare their bodies for the rigors of their game. Size will increase and speed of movement should be improved. Plan 4 is aimed at improving cardiovascular fitness and building muscle endurance. If you are not on an aerobic exercise program of some type, Plan 4 is best for you.

Other than the latter recommendation, I can't tell you which of the four plans to select. That's up to you. Regardless of the program you select, you are to train three or four days a week with at least one full day of rest between exercise sessions. You can work out on a Monday/Wednesday/Friday/Sunday schedule or a Saturday/Tuesday/Thursday/Saturday combination. Regardless of the days, do not skip the day of rest. The safest and most effective way to build your body through free-weight training requires that you allow your muscles to rest at least one full day between exercise sessions. The single exception to this would be if you worked your upper body one day and your lower body the next day. That way you could exercise daily.

It's also a good idea to exercise at a certain time each day to guarantee that you will stick to your program. We are all creatures of habit. There are, however, two times to avoid training with free weights—immediately before going to bed and within an hour after eating a full meal.

THE FOUR PLANS

Let's proceed with the four plans of training with free weights.

PLAN 1: EXERCISING FOR MUSCLE ENDURANCE, APPEARANCE, AND DEFINITION

If your body is not what you want it to be in terms of shape, firmness, and attractiveness, then this plan is best for you. It is designed to build your physique without building bulk. Here, you will lift lighter weights, but you will repeat each lift more times than you would if you were following Plan 2 or 3.

PLAN 2: EXERCISING FOR STRENGTH AND BULK

If your body is deficient in overall strength or you want to put on muscle, then Plan 2 is for you. This program focuses on building muscle groups so they become stronger and bigger. You lift heavy weights a few times.

PLAN 3: EXERCISING FOR POWER, SPORT, AND BULK

Power includes strength along with speed—two essential ingredients in sport. Therefore, with this combination approach, you are building power. It means that you lift heavier weights but at a much faster rate of speed than if you were following Plan 1 or 2.

PLAN 4: AEROBIC WEIGHT TRAINING

Aerobic weight training allows you to build and tone your body as in Plan 1 but at the same time increase your aerobic capacity by 5–7 percent. If you are dissatisfied with your cardiovascular fitness and you're not into running, bicycling, swimming, or other types of aerobic exercise—but you *are* interested in weights—this is best for you.

Take some time now to review in your mind what objective you want to accomplish—definition, bulk or strength, power for sport and bulk, or definition and aerobic power.

THE CORE EXERCISES

The core exercises are your beginning exercises. Stay with these for at least three, and preferably six, months. These exercises will strengthen, firm, and condition the major muscle groups of your body.

While there are 15 core exercises, 11 are considered best for men and 12 for women. This is because the two sexes have different basic figure and/or fitness faults and because men and women seem to prefer different exercises. The table on page 44 lists the core exercises for the women and for the men. To do the 11 or 12 exercises as described in Chapter 6 will take you 60 minutes or so. If the number of exercises and minutes of exercise are more than you bargained for, select only those core exercises that affect your major fitness or figure faults. A minimum of four exercises should be selected.

THE CORRECT POUNDAGE

Once you have established the number of lifts, it is necessary to decide how many pounds you should lift for each exercise. The best approach is to spend three to seven days working on the 11 or 12 exercises. Practice the lifts. Get a feel for your newfound sport and weights. During this three- to seven-day period, establish your

Core Exercises for Men and for Women

EXERCISE	WOMEN	MEN	BODY PART
Arm Press	Yes	Yes	Shoulder/Upper Back
Shoulder Shrug		Yes	Shoulder/Upper Back
Bench Press	Yes	Yes	Chest
Supine Pullover	Yes		Chest
Barbell Curl	Yes	Yes	Arms
Side Sit-Up	Yes	Yes	Waist
Dumbbell Curl-Down	Yes	Yes	Abdomen
Sit-Up	Yes	Yes	Abdomen
Fire Hydrant	Yes		Hips
Leg Extension	Yes		Buttocks
Sprinter		Yes	Buttocks
Plié	Yes		Inner Thigh
Half Squat or Walking Squat		Yes	Thigh
Knee Curl	Yes	Yes	Hamstring
Single-Calf Raise	Yes	Yes	Calf

maximum lift for each particular exercise. Your Arm Curl maximum may be 40 pounds; your Arm Press may be 50 pounds; etc. Obviously, there will be different poundages for each exercise. Regardless of the poundage, record these as your starting weights or pounds.

Once your maximum poundage has been established, it's time to determine your appropriate training weight. If muscle definition is your goal, you are to train at 20–40 percent of your maximum. Therefore, if you can curl a maximum of 50 pounds, your training weight would be 10–20 pounds. If your goal is strength or bulk, you are to train at 50–80 percent of your maximum lift. With the 50-pound example, you would be lifting 25–40 pounds.

See the table on page 45 for a summary of approximate training poundages for the various training plans. These percentages are only guidelines, but they apply to most people. Just remember to listen to your body. If the training weights seem too light or too heavy, adjust them accordingly.

Summary of Training Poundage

GOAL	PERCENTAGE OF MAXIMUM POUNDAGE FOR TRAINING*
Definition (Endurance)	20%-40%
Bulk (Strength)	50%-80%
Sport (Power)	40%-60%
Aerobic (Cardiovascular)	20%-30%

* As a rough rule of thumb, younger, better-conditioned trainers should start at the high percentages. The older or more poorly conditioned people should start with the lower percentages.

Below, record the exercises you have selected, your maximum poundage lifted, and the appropriate percentage of weight to be lifted during training.

Your Personal Training Schedule

Exercises	Maximum Poundage	Training Poundage *
1._____	____pounds	____pounds
2._____	____pounds	____pounds
3._____	____pounds	____pounds
4._____	____pounds	____pounds
5._____	____pounds	____pounds
6._____	____pounds	____pounds
7._____	____pounds	____pounds
8._____	____pounds	____pounds
9._____	____pounds	____pounds
10._____	____pounds	____pounds
11._____	____pounds	____pounds
12._____	____pounds	____pounds

* 20%-40% of maximum for definition/endurance
  50%-80% of maximum for bulk/strength
  40%-60% of maximum for sport/bulk/power
  20%-30% of maximum for aerobic capacity

It may take you several days to determine your best training weight for each of the 11 or 12 exercises. This time is well spent. You will become familiar with the weights, and your muscles will become better conditioned. Don't be impatient to get on with your plan.

Once you have established the poundage for each of your exercises, you are ready to begin training seriously. The only question that remains is the number of repetitions you are to do. That is described below under each of the four plans.

The procedure for three of the four plans with free weights is quite simple. Select Plan 1, 2, or 3 and then do the specified number of repetitions for each lift three times (three sets). Over the weeks, do not proceed to a higher weight until you are able to perform three sets of the specified number of repetitions—that is, 8 or 15. When you are able to do three complete sets of repetitions for an exercise, you may add more weight and start the cycle once more for that lift. Plan 4 requires a special approach and is described below.

PLAN 1: EXERCISING FOR MUSCLE ENDURANCE, APPEARANCE, AND DEFINITION

SCHEDULE

Three exercise sessions a week, with at least one day of rest between each session. All exercises selected (minimum of four) are to be done at each session.

OVERLOAD

Training weights are 20–40 percent of your maximum for each exercise. Therefore, if you tested out at 100 pounds for a particular exercise, you will be training with 20–40 pounds. Start out on the low side if you are unfit, on the high side if you are in good physical condition. Do the exercise 15 times, rest, and repeat two more times—that is, three sets of 15 repetitions each.

PROGRAM

1. Lifting the training weight, you should be able to perform a maximum of 15 repetitions. You're not racing against time, but the repetitions must be done in a consecutive fashion. If you are able to do more than 15 repetitions, the weight is not heavy enough. If you cannot do 15 repetitions, the weight is too heavy. Adjust the weight upward or downward accordingly.

2. Rest one minute after the 15 repetitions. A good way to relax is simply to shake your arms and legs.
3. Repeat the 15 repetitions—no more. Because of fatigue from the previous 15 repetitions, you'll probably be able to do somewhere between 10 and 12 repetitions.
4. Rest one minute.
5. Repeat the exercise. Again, because of fatigue from the previous two sets, now you will probably be able to do somewhere between 7 and 10 repetitions.
6. After a rest of 1½-2 minutes, proceed to the next exercise in your program, following the same procedure for each exercise.

ADAPTATION AND PROGRESSION

In one to three weeks, your body will adapt to the overload of the weight and repetitions. When you can do 15 repetitions of each of the three sets for *any* given exercise, add 2½-5 pounds to the barbell or dumbbell and repeat the cycle of attempting three sets of 15 repetitions each for each exercise. After several weeks, when you are able to do three sets of 15, again increase the weight by 2½-5 pounds. After several months of training, the increments of increase may be only 1-2 pounds.

PLAN 2: EXERCISING FOR STRENGTH AND BULK

SCHEDULE

Three exercise sessions a week, with at least one day of rest between each session. All exercises selected (minimum of four) are to be done at each session.

OVERLOAD

Training weights are 50-80 percent of your maximum for the entire exercise. Therefore, if you tested out at 100 pounds for a particular exercise, you will be training with 50-80 pounds. Start out with the lower weights if you are unfit, the higher if you are in good physical condition. Do the exercises eight times, rest, and repeat two more times—that is, three sets of eight repetitions each.

PROGRAM

1. Perform eight repetitions of each exercise at a rate you feel is comfortable. Speed is not important. Your goal is eight repetitions, maximum. If you can do more, the weight is not heavy enough. If you cannot do eight, you'll have to reduce the weight.
2. Rest one minute.
3. Attempt eight more repetitions of the exercise. Because of fatigue from the previous eight repetitions, you'll probably be able to do only five or six repetitions.
4. Rest one minute.
5. Repeat the exercise. Again, because of fatigue from the previous two sets of repetitions, you'll probably be able to do only three to five repetitions.
6. After a rest of 1½–2 minutes, proceed to the next exercise in your program, following the same procedure for each exercise.

ADAPTATION AND PROGRESSION

In one to three weeks, your body will adapt to the overload of weight and repetitions. When you can do eight repetitions in each of the three sets for *any* given exercise, add 2½–5 pounds to the barbell or dumbbell. Repeat the cycle of attempting three sets of repetitions for each exercise. After several weeks, when you are able to do three sets of eight, again increase the weight by 2½–5 pounds. After several months of training, the increments of increase may be only 1–2 pounds.

PLAN 3: EXERCISING FOR POWER, SPORT, AND BULK

SCHEDULE

Three exercise sessions a week, with at least one day of rest between each session. All exercises selected (minimum of four) are to be done at each session.

OVERLOAD

Training weights are 40–60 percent of your maximum for each exercise. Therefore, if you tested out at 100 pounds for a particular exercise, you will be training with 40-60 pounds. Start out with the lower weight if you are unfit, the higher if you are in good physical condition. Do the exercise eight times, rest, and repeat two more times—that is, three sets of eight repetitions each.

PROGRAM

1. Perform eight repetitions of each exercise within a time period not to exceed 10-12 seconds (the shorter the better). *Be cautious: because of the need to do the exercises in a specified period of time, there will be a tendency to cheat. Do the exercise correctly. You must go through the full range of motion for each repetition.* If you can do more than eight repetitions in that period of time, the weight is not heavy enough. If you cannot perform the eight repetitions, though, you must reduce the weight.
2. Rest one minute.
3. Attempt eight more repetitions of the exercise in 10-12 seconds. Because of fatigue from the previous eight repetitions, you'll probably be able to do only five to seven repetitions.
4. Rest one minute.
5. Repeat the exercise. Again, because of fatigue from the previous two sets of repetitions, you'll probably be able to do only four to seven repetitions within the 10- to 12-second time limit.
6. After a rest of 1½-2 minutes, proceed to the next exercise in your program and follow the same procedure for each exercise.

ADAPTATION AND PROGRESSION

In one to three weeks, your body will adapt to the overload of weight, repetitions, and time. When you can do eight repetitions in 10-12 seconds or less in each of the three sets for any given exercise, add 2½-5 pounds to the barbell or dumbbells. Repeat the cycle of attempting three sets of eight repetitions of each exercise in the allotted time. After several weeks, when you are able to do three sets of eight repetitions, increase the weight by 2½-5 pounds. After several months of training, the increments of increase may be only 1-2 pounds.

PLAN 4: AEROBIC WEIGHT TRAINING

SCHEDULE

Three exercise sessions a week, with at least one day of rest between each session. All exercises selected (minimum of 10) are to be done at each session.

OVERLOAD

Training weights are 20–30 percent of your maximum for each exercise. Therefore, if you tested out at 100 pounds for a particular exercise, you will be training with 20–30 pounds. Start with the lower weights if you are unfit, the higher if you are in good physical condition. You will go through the circuit of 10 exercises at least three times.

PROGRAM

1. Incorporate activities other than the exercises with free weights. Activities such as running in place, rope skipping, rebounding, riding a stationary bicycle, stair climbing, and bench stepping are appropriate.
2. Do the exercises with free weights rapidly. Perform them at a high intensity, emphasizing speed.
3. The combination of free-weight exercise and additional activities should be strenuous enough to increase your heart rate to your training heart rate level (see page 51).
4. The exercises should be arranged in such a way that they don't overstress one part of the body. In other words, you don't want to work the same muscle groups or body parts two times in a row. You might start with the upper third, followed by a middle-third exercise, and then do the lower third. After that, repeat the cycle.
5. The number of repetitions you are to do for each free weight exercise is 15.
6. Usually, circuits are performed in three- to five-lap dosages. A lap is one complete circuit of the 10 free weight exercises plus the cardiovascular conditioning exercises.

   Once you've got your poundage straightened out, it's time to see how long it takes you to do the entire circuit of 10 free

Your Training Heart Rate and Heart Rate Range

AGE	YOUR MAXIMUM HEART RATE *	YOUR TRAINING HEART RATE **	YOUR TRAINING HEART RATE RANGE ***
20	200	150	140-170
25	195	146	137-166
30	190	142	133-162
35	185	139	130-157
40	180	135	126-153
45	175	131	123-149
50	170	127	119-145
55	165	124	116-140
60	160	120	112-136
65	155	116	109-132
70	150	112	105-128

* Beats per minute ** 75% of the maximum in beats per minute *** 70%-85% of the maximum in beats per minute

To read this chart, find the age closest to yours at the far left. Then read across the page to find your training heart rate range. Therefore, a 50-year-old, who has a maximum heart rate of 170 beats per minute, should train at a heart rate of 119-145 beats per minute. Use the low side if you are unfit, the high side if you are in good physical condition.

HEART RATE

The number of times your heart pumps blood each minute is your pulse rate or heart rate. To feel your pulse, turn the palm of your hand up and place two or three fingers of your right hand on the thumb side of your left wrist. This point is called the *radial pulse.*

When taking your pulse, you should feel a push or thump against you fingers. Each push is one beat of your heart. This beat is called your *pulse.* The number of pushes each minute is your heart or pulse rate. If you have trouble locating your radial pulse, place your first two fingers on one side of your throat just below the point of the jaw and locate the carotid artery. As you do this, press lightly. Avoid pressing too hard when checking a carotid pulse.

After locating your pulse, look at the sweep second hand on your watch. Starting with zero, count the number of beats for a 10-second interval. Multiply that number by six. This represents your resting heart rate per minute.

weight exercises plus the accompanying aerobic exercises. So, do three to five laps (you choose the number of laps). Once you've established how long it takes you to do three, four, or five laps, reduce this time by 25 percent to get your target time, which is your goal. Reach for your goal over the next three to four weeks. For example, let's say it took you 15 minutes and 30 seconds to complete a three-lap circuit of 10 exercises and rope jumping 25 times between each exercise. Your target time would be about 11 minutes and 30 seconds.

ADAPTATION AND PROGRESSION

As your physical condition improves, your body will adapt to the demand placed on it. You will be able to do the exercises faster and improve in skill and physical condition.

Once you reach your goal, progressively add to the circuit in the following manner:

1. Do an additional lap of your circuit.
2. Increase the repetitions of each exercise you include.
3. Lengthen the duration of aerobic work between exercises.
4. Change the exercises to a more strenuous form. For example, modifying the Push-Up might mean that you perform Bent-Knee Push-Ups, then Full-Length Push-Ups, and then Full-Length Push-Ups with a Hand Clap, and finally Push-Ups from a Handstand.

The box on page 53 provides a sample aerobic circuit. The various exercises used are described in Chapter 6.

The above circuit is designed to work different muscle groups. It begins with an exercise that works the upper body, followed by the middle third and then the lower third of the body. Do the exercises in the sequence shown. More difficult exercises can be done later. Do not exercise the same area of your body or the same muscle groups consecutively. Once you have completed exercise 10, you are finished with one lap. Then begin the second lap with exercise 1. A full circuit would consist of three to five laps.

MODEL AEROBIC CIRCUIT

1. Arm Press—15 repetitions, followed by 25 repetitions of running in place or jumping rope.
2. Curl—15 repetitions, followed by 25 repetitions of jumping rope or jumping jacks or running in place.
3. One-Half Squat—15 repetitions, followed by jumping rope or running in place for 25 repetitions.
4. Barbell Curls—15 repetitions, followed by jumping rope or running in place for 25 repetitions.
5. Curl and Cross-Touch—15 repetitions, followed by jumping rope or running in place for 25 repetitions.
6. Lunge—15 repetitions, followed by jumping rope or running in place for 25 repetitions.
7. Forward Raise—15 repetitions, followed by jumping rope or running in place for 25 repetitions.
8. Side Sit-Up—15 repetitions, followed by jumping rope or running in place for 25 repetitions.
9. Calf Raise—15 repetitions, followed by jumping rope or running in place for 25 repetitions.
10. French Press—15 repetitions, followed by jumping rope or running in place for 25 repetitions.

6

THE EXERCISES

ON THE FOLLOWING pages are 48 exercises to be used for conditioning the body. Naturally, not all of these exercises should be done; a variety is provided to give you some choices.

I do suggest, however, that at the start of your training you stay with 11–12 of the 15 exercises noted with an asterisk (*). These are considered the core exercises. After three to six months of training, and as you become more familiar with free weights and your body becomes better conditioned, you will seek variety. Then it is OK to select other exercises from the general groups.

Before you begin the free-weight exercises, be sure to warm up.

EXERCISES FOR WARMING UP

Most athletes warm up before a game or contest. If you go to a baseball game, you'll see the players warming up outside the dugout—stretching or bending, maybe even running. At a track and field event, you will see some of the runners jogging around the track or stretching carefully and deliberately while waiting to perform. These are not just idle activities. Athletes know that, if they are to perform well, they must prepare their muscular, skeletal, and cardiovascular systems for more demanding exercise.

Training with free weights is a physical activity well suited to pre- and post-exercise workouts. Because it is vigorous, free-weight training places stress on the body. In order to withstand these demands, muscles must be stretched and warmed up. Heart rate and circulation must be increased. In short, I'm telling you to get your body going before you start to lift weights.

Warming-up exercises are designed to work on the muscles, ligaments, tendons, and joints that absorb the stress of particular free-weight training exercises. The following exercises will ready the heart and lungs, stimulate them, and prepare them to meet more than the usual demands. While training with free weights may not be classified as building cardiovascular endurance, it is important that you recognize that the demands placed on the cardiovascular system when lifting are great.

In reality, warming up means getting the oxygen-carrying blood flowing strongly to the muscles to be exercised. There are two effective methods of warming up: loosening-up calisthenics and light weight workouts. Do both prior to lifting. If you are pressed for time, one will do, but for a complete workout the two are recommended.

Again, a particular number of warm-up exercises is not specified. Instead, I recommend that you warm up regularly before you start any weight-training program, devoting a period of 5–10 minutes to your warm-up. Warm up for 5 minutes if you are rather young (under 21), and 10 minutes if you're 30 or older. Feel free to pick the exercises that you want to do. Be sure to tie your warm-ups into the free weight training that will follow. For example, if your free weight program emphasizes the upper-body muscles, make sure that you warm up these muscles.

The following exercises are divided into two categories—loosening up and light weight workouts. Start with the loosening-up exercises and progress to the light weight workouts.

LOOSENING-UP EXERCISES

All of the following exercises are to be done while you are walking or walking in place.

Walk—Alternate High Arm
Swings.

Walk—Alternate Swings.

Walk—Backstroke
(Backward Crawl).

Walk—Alternate High Arm Swings. Improves shoulder
flexibility.
1. Swing the arms alternately forward and back. The hands
should reach at least shoulder height on the forward swing.
Walk—Alternate Swings.
1. Raise both arms above the head while walking.
2. Rotate one arm in one direction and the other in the opposite
direction.
Walk—Backstroke (Backward Crawl). Improves shoulder
flexibility.
1. Alternately, swing right and left arms upward, backward,
and around, simulating the swimming backstroke.

Walk—Double Arm Pumps.

Walk—Clasp Hands
Overhead and Bend.

Walk—Cross-Body Arm
Swings.

Walk—Cross-Body Arm Swings. Helps to prevent a round-shouldered appearance.

1. Swing both arms across the body, then reverse the action by swinging both arms sideward and back as far as possible. Keep the hands at chest height.

Walk—Clasp Hands Overhead and Bend. Helps to stretch the lateral muscles of the trunk.

1. While walking, clasp the hands overhead.
2. Bend alternately to the left and right.

Walk—Double-Arm Pumps. Pumping action helps to massage the blood vessels, thereby promoting circulatory stimulation. By stretching the muscles of the chest, this exercise also helps to prevent a round-shouldered appearance.

1. Swing both arms forward and back simultaneously along the sides of the body.
2. On the forward swings, flex both arms, draw the fist in toward the shoulders, and pump twice.

Walk—Double Arm Swings
Forward and Back.

Walk—Forward Crawl.

Walk—Giant Arm Circles
Backward.

Walk—Double-Arm Swings Forward and Back. Improves shoulder flexibility.
1. Swing both arms forward and backward together while walking.
2. As the arms swing forward, they should come up alongside the ears.
3. As they swing backward, they should go slightly behind the body.

Walk—Forward Crawl. Improves shoulder flexibility.
1. While walking, swing the right and left arms alternately up overhead and down in front of the body, simulating the swimming forward crawl.

Walk—Giant Arm Circles Backward. Stretches and improves the flexibility of the muscles of the chest and shoulders.
1. Swing the arms in a complete circle, upward and across in front of the body and then backward and around.

Knee Hug.

Walk—Upper Twist.

Walk—High Arm
Crossovers.

Walk—High Arm Crossovers. Improves shoulder flexibility.
1. Reach overhead and cross the hands.
2. Then bring the arms down alongside the body to the hips.
3. Repeat.
Walk—Upper Twist. Improves trunk flexibility.
1. While walking, twist the upper part of your body from left to right.
Knee Hug. Lightly stretches the seat muscles.
1. While walking, take three steps and raise the right knee to your chest, assisting with both hands.
2. Return your right foot to the floor and repeat for the left leg.
3. Continue.

Light-weight workout,
upper body.

Light-weight workout,
middle body.

Light-weight workout,
lower body.

LIGHT WEIGHT WORKOUTS

After the loosening-up exercises, it is a good idea to do a series of
lifts with lighter weights than you intend to use during the heavy
lifting. Do not use more than half the weight you plan to use in the
"heavy" phase of lifting and do no more than half the repetitions.
You can, of course, individualize your efforts, as long as your
workout is comfortable and free of strain. Remember, all you want
to do is loosen up the muscles—the actual free-weight training
exercise comes later. You don't have to use all the lifts in this
instance. These warm-up lifts are appropriate—one for the upper
third of your body, one for the middle, and one for the lower.

After the loosening-up exercises and the light weight workouts, you are ready to move into your free-weight training plan (Plans 1–4).

FREE WEIGHT EXERCISES

NECK

Neck Curl. Develops and firms muscles on the front of the neck and provides a more attractive neckline.
1. Lie on your back with the legs bent. Hold the weight (plate) on forehead with both hands.
2. Curl the head forward. Most people can curl four inches or so.
3. Slowly return to the starting position. That is one repetition.
4. Repeat.

Neck Extension. Develops muscles on the back of the neck and helps provide a flaring and more attractive neckline.
1. Lie on your stomach with face on the floor, legs and toes touching the floor, and one arm extended. Hold the weight (plate) on back of head.
2. Lift head slowly backward and upward as high as possible. For most people, this is about four inches. Do not raise the chest off the floor.
3. Slowly return to the starting position. That is one repetition.
4. Repeat.

Neck Lift (Side). Develops the muscles on the front and back of the neck and helps develop a more attractive neckline.
1. Lie on right side, head resting on the outstretched right arm. Hold weight (plate) on the side of the head.
2. Lift head upward and sideward as far as possible. For most people, this is four inches or so.
3. Slowly return to the original position. That is one repetition.
4. Repeat.
5. Do on the other side.

Neck Curl.

Neck Extension.

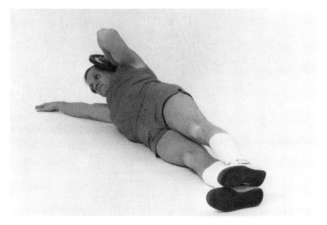

Neck Lift.

SHOULDERS AND UPPER BACK

*Arm Press. Develops and firms muscles of the shoulders, upper back, upper chest, and back of the upper arms. Aids in the prevention of round shoulders.

1. Stand with feet shoulder width apart. Hold barbell in front of the chest with an overhand grip, hands slightly more than shoulder width apart.
2. Extend barbell overhead until arms are straight.
3. Return barbell to the starting position. That is one repetition.
4. Repeat.

Dumbbell Row. Develops and firms muscles in the front of the arms, the forearms, shoulders, and upper back.

1. Stand in a short forward-lunge position. Rest your hand on the forward thigh for support. Hold the dumbbell in opposite hand, hanging straight down from the shoulder.
2. Bend the elbow to bring the weight up toward the armpit, then slowly straighten arm downward to return to the starting position. That is one repetition.
3. Repeat.
4. Repeat on the other side.

Lateral Raise. Develops and firms the muscles of the shoulders (traps and delts) and helps provide an attractive shoulder line.

1. Stand with feet hip width apart, toes pointed outward slightly. Hold dumbbells down at the sides of your body in overhand grip.
2. Keeping the arms straight, lift the dumbbells sideways until arms are parallel to floor or beyond, preferably until your arms form a *V* (about a 45-degree angle above the horizontal).
3. Return to the starting position. That is one repetition.
4. Repeat.

*Shoulder Shrug. Develops and firms the shoulder muscles (traps and delts) and provides for a more attractive shoulder line.

1. Stand with feet waist width apart, arms extended downward. Hold barbell in overhand grip, hands at sides of the thighs (or hands resting on thighs), barbell resting against the thighs.
2. Keeping the arms straight, lift the shoulders upward as far as possible.
3. Return to the starting position. That is one repetition.
4. Repeat.

Arm Press.   Dumbbell Row.   Lateral Raise.

Shoulder Shrug.   Punching Bag.

Punching Bag. Develops and firms the muscles of the middle and upper back. Provides for a more attractive back in relationship to the waist. Also works on shoulders, front of upper arms, and back of upper arms.

1. Bend forward at the waist until your upper body is parallel to the floor. Keep your knees bent slightly. Hold a dumbbell in each hand.
2. From this position, extend one arm forward and pull the other arm back, elbow up, to your waist.
3. Punch forward with the bent arm until it is fully extended; simultaneously pull the opposite arm back. That is one repetition.
4. Repeat.

Note: Your movement should be rapid and fluid.

CHEST

*Bench Press. Develops and firms muscles of the chest, back of the upper arms, and shoulders.

1. Lie on your back on a flat exercise bench, knees bent and feet on the floor. The barbell is supported on a weight rack or held by a partner. Grasp the barbell with an overhand grip, arms fully extended, hands shoulder width apart.
2. Lower the barbell to touch your chest.
3. Press the barbell back to the starting position. That is one repetition.
4. Repeat.

Forward Raise. Develops and firms muscles of the upper chest and shoulders.

1. Stand with your feet waist width apart. Hold dumbbells down at the sides of your body (or resting on your thighs) in an overhand grip.
2. Raise the dumbbells forward to shoulder height, keeping the arms straight.
3. Lower the dumbbells to the original position. That is one repetition.
4. Repeat.

Variation: Do one arm at a time.

Pectoral Fly (Standing). Develops and firms chest and shoulder muscles.

1. Stand with your feet waist width apart, toes pointed outward slightly, and hold dumbbells out to the sides with elbows bent so that together the arms form a *U*.
2. Keeping arms in this bent position, move them horizontally toward the center of your body until dumbbells touch.
3. Open arms horizontally out to the sides to return to the starting position. That is one repetition.
4. Repeat.

*Supine Pullover. Develops and firms muscles in the front of the chest, back of the upper arms, and sides of the chest.

1. Assume a supine position on the floor, knees bent, and arms extended out beyond the head parallel to the body. Hold the barbell with an overhand grip.
2. Raise arms to a 90-degree angle directly overhead; keep the arms straight.

Bench Press.

Forward Raise.   Pectoral Fly (Standing).

Supine Pull-Over.

3. Return the barbell to the original position, keeping the arms straight. That is one repetition.

4. Repeat.

*Barbell Curl. Develops and firms the muscles of the upper arms and the forearms.

1. Stand with feet apart, arms at sides. Hold the barbell against the thighs in an underhand grip.

2. Flex forearms, raising the barbell to the shoulders.

3. Return to the starting position. This is one repetition.

4. Repeat.

French Press. Develops and firms the muscles on the back of the arms and shoulders.

1. Stand with your feet shoulder width apart and your body erect. Hold a dumbbell by one end in both hands with your arms fully extended overhead.

2. Lower the dumbbell behind your head as far as possible by bending the elbows.

3. Raise the weight back to the starting position. That is one repetition.

4. Repeat.

Note: Remember to keep the elbows pointed straight up and close to your head throughout the movement.

Wrist Curl. Develops and firms the muscles of the forearms.

1. Sit on a bench, forearms resting on thighs, and the wrists extending beyond the knees. Hold the barbell in an underhand grip.

2. Extend the hands at the wrists and lower the bar as far as possible toward the floor.

3. Flex the wrists, bring the bar upward as far as possible, and return to the starting position. That is one repetition.

4. Repeat.

Wrist Extensor. Develops and firms the muscles of the forearms.

1. Sit on a bench, forearms resting on your thighs, wrists extended beyond the knees. Hold the barbell in an overhand grip.

2. Lift the bar by extending the wrists upward through their maximum range of motion. Do not lift your forearms.

3. Return to the starting position. That is one repetition.

4. Repeat.

Barbell Curl.

French Press.

Wrist Curl.

Wrist Extensor.

WAIST

Side Double-Leg Raise. Firms the muscles of the waist.
1. Lie on your right side, right arm extended above your head, palm on the floor, head resting on the extended arm.
2. Keeping your legs together and straight, raise them off the floor.
3. Lower your legs to the starting position. That is one repetition.
4. Repeat.
5. Do on the other side.

Knee Drop—Side. Firms the waist and abdomen.
1. Lie on your back with weights on ankles and arms at the sides.
2. Bring your knees to your chest.
3. Lower bent legs to the left side, then to your right side, but do not let them touch the floor. That is one repetition.
4. Repeat.
Note: Keep both arms on the floor throughout the movement.

*Side Sit-Up. Firms the muscles of the waist.
1. Lie on your side, body straight, hands clasped behind the neck.
2. Have a partner hold your feet down for support or put them under a loaded barbell.
3. Raise your upper body off the floor, bending directly toward your side. Slowly lower back down. That is one repetition.
4. Repeat.
5. Do on the other side.

Twist. Firms the muscles of the waist.
1. Sit straight on a bench with an unloaded barbell held across the back of your shoulders.
2. Twist your upper torso to the right.
3. Twist your upper torso to the left. That is one repetition.
4. Repeat.

Curl. Firms the abdominal muscles.
1. Lie flat on your back, knees bent, hands and arms off the floor but parallel to it.
2. Tighten your abdominal muscles and push the small of your back into the floor.
3. Bring your knees to your chest, simultaneously tucking your chin down into your chest, and curl upward as far as possible.

Side Double-Leg Riase.

Knee Drop—Side.

Side Sit-Ups.

Twist.

Curl.

Curl and Cross Touch.

Return. That is one repetition.

4. Repeat.

Curl and Cross-Touch. Firms the abdominal muscles.

1. Lie flat on your back, knees bent, hands placed along neck, and elbows bent.

2. Tighten the abdominal muscles and push the small of the back into the floor.

3. Bring your left foot off the floor so that the lower leg is parallel to the floor. Simultaneously curl upward and touch your right elbow to the inside of the left knee. Return. That is one repetition.

4. Repeat with the left elbow to right knee.

*Dumbbell Curl-Down. Firms abdominal, waist, and neck muscles.
1. Sit with the feet on the floor, knees bent. Hold the dumbbells in front of the neck and elbows bent at about 90 degrees.
2. Lower your upper body backward toward the floor. Hold at this point (do not lower the shoulders and head to the floor).
3. Curl upward again until sitting upright. That is one repetition.
4. Repeat.

Note: If you have back problems, go all the way to the floor but avoid sitting up again.

Knee to Chest. Firms abdominal muscles.
1. Lie on your back, hands interlocked behind the head.
2. Bend the knees and bring as close to the chest as possible while simultaneously raising your shoulders off the floor.
3. Return to the starting position and repeat on the other side. That is one repetition.
4. Repeat.

Note: Ankle weights may be worn.

V-Seat. Firms abdominal muscles.
1. Sit on the floor with your legs straight, ankles together, and your palms on the floor behind you for support.
2. Bend your knees to your chest.
3. Straighten your legs in midair. Return to the starting position. That is one repetition.
4. Repeat.

Note: Ankle weights may be worn.

Single-Leg Raise. Firms the abdominal muscles.
1. Lie flat on your back, one leg bent and one extended, hands at your sides as illustrated.
2. Tighten your abdominal muscles and flatten the small of your back into the floor.
3. Keep the knee of your straight leg tight and raise this leg slowly to the level of the bent knee, as illustrated. Return. That is one repetition.
4. Repeat this movement with each leg.

Note: Ankle weights may be worn.

*Sit-Up. Firms muscles of the abdomen.
1. Lie flat on your back, knees bent, hands and arms off the floor and parallel to it.

Dumbbell Curl-Down.

Knee to Chest.

V-Seat.

Single-Leg Raise.

Sit-Up.

2. Tighten abdominal muscles and push small of the back into the floor.
3. Curl up slowly until your shoulder blades clear the floor. Stop there, hold momentarily, then return yourself to the floor. That is one repetition.
4. Repeat.

HIPS

*Fire Hydrant. Firms muscles of the hips and the saddle bags.
1. Get on your hands and knees, wearing ankle weights.
2. Extend one leg out to the side, keeping the knee bent.
3. Lift the leg up high and then return to the starting position. That is one repetiton.
4. Repeat with the other leg.

Hip Abductor. Develops and firms the muscles on the side of the hips and the saddle bags.
1. Wear ankle weights. Lie on one side with the low arm extended above the head, the top arm across the front of the body for support.
2. Raise the top leg as far as possible, working toward an angle of 45 degrees or more.
3. Slowly lower the leg to the original position. (Keep the knee extended at all times during the movement.) That is one repetition.
4. Repeat the exercise on the other side with the other leg.

Kneeling Leg Lateral. Firms the hip and saddle bag muscles.
1. Kneel on all fours, wearing ankle or lace weights, and extend one leg out to the side as far as possible, keeping the knee straight and foot flexed.
2. Lift your leg up to a point where the leg is parallel to the floor.
3. Return leg to the floor and keep the leg turned forward. That is one repetition.
4. Repeat with the other leg.

Note: Only the leg should move.

Side Kick. Firms the hip and saddle bag muscles.
1. Wear ankle or lace weights. Start with the hands on the hips. Stand straight with the abdomen in, shoulders back. Keep good posture throughout the movement.
2. Extend the right leg out to the side as far as possible without bending the knee, keeping the foot flexed.
3. Hold. Then bring the leg down.
4. Repeat with the other leg. That is one repetition.

Note: This exercise can be done in an alternating fashion so that it's Hip Kicks from left to right.

Fire Hydrant.

Hip Abductor.

Kneeling Leg Lateral.

Side Kick.

BUTTOCKS

Bent-Over Leg Raise. Firms the buttocks.

1. Wearing ankle or lace weights, bend at the waist from a standing position, resting hands on the floor and keeping both legs straight throughout the exercise.
2. Lift the left leg straight back and up high, keeping the foot flexed. Keep the foot pointed toward the floor. *Do not arch your back.*
3. Keep your head lowered and return. That is one repetition.
4. Repeat with the other leg.

Kneeling Leg Curl. Firms the buttocks area.

1. Wearing ankle or lace weights, kneel on all fours, with elbows bent and head lower than your buttocks.
2. Extend the leg directly backward, keeping your spine straight at all times, foot flexed, and head down.
3. Bend and straighten the knee, keeping the worked muscles tight; only the lower leg moves. That is one repetition.
4. Repeat with the other leg.

*Leg Extension. Firms the buttocks area.

1. Wearing ankle or lace weights, kneel down and bring one knee toward your chest, keeping your head down.
2. Kick the leg back, raising your head slightly. Leg and head should be parallel with the back; no hyperextension.
3. Bring the knee forward to the chest again. Repeat. That is one repetition.
4. Repeat with the other leg.

*Sprinter. Firms the buttocks.

1. Wearing ankle or lace weights, assume a position on all fours in a long sprinter's position. One knee should be bent close to your chest, the other leg straight out in back of your body. Arms should be straight under your shoulders.
2. Take long strides in a bounding motion, alternating position of legs. When both the left and right leg have been fully extended once, that is one repetition.

Note: If you have a history of knee problems, avoid this exercise.

Bent-Over Leg Raise.

Kneeling Leg Curl.

Leg Extension.

Sprinter.

LOWER THIRD—INNER THIGH

*Plie. Firms the inner thighs and buttocks.

1. Stand with your legs far apart and feet turned outward approximately 45 degrees. Balance a barbell across the back of your shoulders and keep your back straight throughout the exercise.
2. Lower your body until the thighs are parallel to the floor.
3. Return. That is one repetition.
4. Repeat.

Note: Your movement should be slow and controlled. Do not bounce. Keep the feet flat on the floor.

Standing Hip Abductor. Firms the muscles of the inner thighs.

1. Stand erect, feet shoulder width apart, wearing ankle or lace weights. Hold on to a table or wall for support.
2. Gradually move your right leg across in front of your body, past your left leg, and lift as high as possible.
3. Return and repeat. That is one repetition.
4. Repeat on the other side.

Plie.

Standing Hip Abductor.

QUADRICEPS—FRONT OF THE THIGH

Hip Flexor. Develops and firms the muscles on the front of the thighs.

1. Wear ankle or lace weights. Sit at the edge of a table so that it touches the back of the knees. Grasp the edge of the table with the hands.
2. Raise the knee toward the chest as far as possible. Do not bend your body forward or backward.
3. Slowly lower the knee. That is one repetition.
4. Repeat with the other leg.

Lunge. Develops and firms muscles in the front of the thighs and buttocks.

1. Stand erect, feet together, the barbell balanced across the back of your shoulders.
2. Take a giant step forward, bend your knees, and touch your trailing knee to the floor.
3. Push up to the starting position. That is one repetition.
4. Repeat with the opposite leg.

*Half Squat. Develops and firms the muscles in the front of the thighs and lower legs.

1. Stand with the feet spread comfortably.
2. Hold the barbell in an overhand grip behind the neck, resting on the shoulders.
3. Bend the knees to perform a One-Half Squat (thighs no more than parallel to the floor). Return to the starting position. That is one repetition.
4. Repeat.

Sitting Leg Raise. Develops and firms the muscles in the front of the thighs.

1. Wear ankle or lace weights or weighted boots. Sit on the edge of a table with the legs hanging over the edge.
2. Raise one leg to a horizontal position by straightening the knee.
3. Return to the starting position. That is one repetition.
4. Repeat the exercise with the other leg.

*Walking Squat. Develops and firms the muscles of the upper and lower legs.

1. Stand with one foot 12–18 inches in front of the other and hold a barbell in an overhand grip behind the neck, resting on the shoulders.

Hip Flexor.

Lunge.

Half Squat.

Sitting Leg Raise.

Walking Squat.

2. Take one step forward, executing a Half-Knee-Bend (thighs parallel to the floor).
3. Return to the upright position. That is one repetition.
4. Repeat the exercise with the other leg.

BACK OF THIGHS

*Knee Curl. Develops and firms the muscles on the back of the legs.
1. Wear ankle/lace weights or weighted boots. Assume a prone position on a bench or on the floor with the hands extended above the head.
2. Curl one leg upward until your heel touches (or almost touches) the buttocks.
3. Assume the original position. That is one repetition.
4. Repeat the exercise with the other leg.

Knee Flexion. Develops and firms the muscles on the back of the upper thighs.
1. Stand erect. Place an ankle/lace weight or weighted boot on each of the legs. Hold on to a table, wall, or bar for support.
2. Flex your knee so that your lower leg actually curls upward toward your buttocks.
3. Return. That is one repetition.
4. Repeat with the other leg.

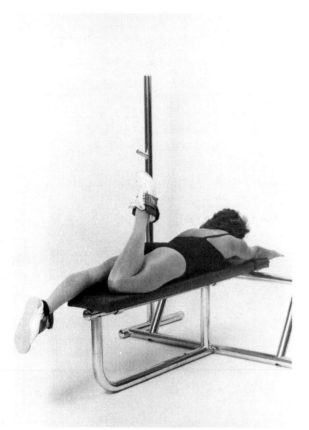

Knee Curl.

Knee Flexion.

LOWER LEGS

Sitting Toe Curl. Develops and firms the muscles on the front of the legs.

1. Wear a weighted boot or lace an ankle weight across the instep of each foot.
2. Sit on a table, legs hanging over the edge of the table.
3. Curl your toes upward as far as possible. Return. That is one repetition.
4. Repeat with the other foot.

Calf Raise. Develops and firms the muscles in the front and the back of the lower legs.

1. Stand with the balls of the feet on a one- to two-inch block of wood or weight plate, with the heels on the floor.
2. Hold the barbell in an overhand grip behind the neck, resting on the shoulders.
3. Rise up on the toes as far as possible. Return to the original position. That is one repetition.
4. Repeat.

*Single Calf Raise. Develops and firms muscles in the back and the front of the lower legs.

1. Stand with the ball of your right foot on a block of wood or weight plate. The top of the left foot should be interlocked behind your right calf.
2. Hold a dumbbell in your right hand.
3. Slowly rise onto your toes as high as possible. Return. That is one repetition.
4. Repeat with the left leg.

Sitting Calf Raise. Develops and firms the muscles on the back of the legs.

1. Sit on a chair and place the balls of your feet on the edge of a book, a block of wood, or a weight plate.
2. Support a weight (dumbbells or barbell) on your knees as illustrated.
3. Push up on your toes as high as possible, lifting the weight upward. Return to the starting position. That is one repetition.
4. Repeat.

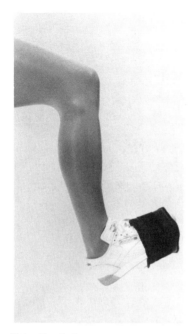

Sitting Toe Curl.

Calf Raise.

Single Calf Raise.

Sitting Calf Raise.

EXERCISES FOR COOLING DOWN

At the conclusion of a free weight training session, you must start to cool down. It is not wise to come to an abrupt halt. For example, runners do a slow lap, and competitive swimmers may take a few laps in the pool. We all know that racehorses need a cool-down period. The cool-down phase is a crucial link between vigorous activity and return to sedentary activity.

Suddenly stopping vigorous exercise can be dangerous because it leaves most of the blood in the wrong place. Sudden relaxation after a demanding session of lifting or other exercise can result in light-headedness, dizziness, nausea, and even fainting or blackout. You have to let your body return to its normal state at a moderate rate. Cooling down or tapering off is a gradual slowing down for maximum (high) muscle contraction to minimum (low) muscle contractions.

When you are exercising vigorously, your heart is pumping blood through its arteries at a faster rate so that it can supply the active muscles with oxygen and life-supporting nutrients. The blood is forcefully pumped to the muscles by the contractions of the heart. There is, however, no similar force to send the blood back from the muscles to the heart by way of the veins. The veins carry the blood back toward the heart.

When you suddenly stop exercising, blood begins to pool in the muscles and veins. When you taper off, however, you prevent the delay in returning blood to the heart, thereby helping the body adjust to the condition of less activity. More blood is directed to the brain, lessening the danger of spasms and cramps in the muscles you have been exercising.

Tapering off helps your body in another way. The fatigue from exercise creates a buildup of lactic acid in the muscles. Cooling off helps to dissipate the lactic acid and therefore eases muscle aches and pains. In addition, tapering off helps your body adjust to weather conditions outside the exercise area. It would be most unwise to go directly from a vigorous exercise session out into the cold, wet weather.

In many ways, the warming up and cooling down of your exercise program are as important as the free weight training itself. Therefore, you should plan to make these activities an integral part of your program. On the following pages are varied cool-down exercises. The variety will keep you from getting bored

and also give you some options for different areas of your body that need work.

After completing a strenuous session with free weights you should keep your body in motion. Walk at a slow pace for three minutes. You may want to lift a light weight several times. Follow up the walking and the light lifting with about 6–10 stretching exercises.

To do the stretching exercises, assume the position called for in the description. Then move in the direction recommended until you feel a "tug" or "pull" on the muscles or a general resistance to stretching further. Hold that position and concentrate on the tug and pull. Visualize the muscle stretching or relaxing. (This may take some real concentration on your part.) As the muscle or tendon relaxes, continue to stretch further until you feel a second tug. Hold that position for 10–20 seconds. Then relax and move on to the next exercise.

When selecting the various exercises, pick a minimum of two for the upper third, two for the middle third, and two for the lower third.

UPPER THIRD

Alternate Reach. Stretches the upper back and shoulders.
1. Assume a bent-knee position while lying on your back.
2. Place one arm above your head with the palm facing up while your other arm is by your side with the palm facing down.
3. Reach in the opposite direction, keeping both arms flat on the floor. Hold the stretch.
4. Change arm positions and repeat.

Elbow Special. Benefits the muscles of your chest and upper back.
1. Stand with your hands behind the head, fingers interlocked.
2. Draw your elbows back as far as possible and hold.
3. Draw the elbows forward and try to touch them together.
4. Hold and repeat.

Kneeling Shoulder Stretch.
1. Kneel on the floor, sit back on your heels, and look at your knees as you reach forward with your hands. Keep your seat down and continue to focus on your knees.
2. Once you have reached as far as possible, press down against the floor with your hands and you will feel your shoulders stretch.
3. Hold and repeat.

Alternate Reach.

Kneeling Shoulder Stretch.

Elbow Special.

Pectoral Stretch. Stretches the chest muscles.
1. Sit with your legs crossed. Place your arms out to the side with the palms facing forward.
2. Push your arms back as far as possible, keeping the arms straight and at shoulder height.
3. Hold and repeat.

Reach for the Sky. Stretches the upper back and shoulders.
1. Kneel with the hands clasped behind the back and the seat resting on the heels. Place your forehead on the ground at the knees.
2. Raise the hands above your back and head as high as possible.
3. Hold and repeat.

Shoulder Squeeze. Stretches the muscles behind your thighs (hamstrings) as well as the back of your arms and shoulders.
1. Stand and hold both hands together behind the back.
2. Bend forward at the waist, keeping the legs straight.
3. Try to raise the arms over the head.
4. Hold and repeat.

Pectoral Stretch.

Reach for the Sky.

Shoulder Squeeze.

MIDDLE THIRD

Knee Raises. Stretches your gluteus maximus.
1. Lie on your back with legs bent.
2. Hold the right knee with both hands and pull the knee toward your chest.
3. Hold and repeat with the left knee.

Side Stretch.
1. Stand with feet shoulder width apart, legs straight. Place one hand on hip and extend other hand up and over head.
2. Bend to the side on which hand is on hip. Move slowly. Hold 6-10 seconds.
3. Repeat on the other side.

Single-Leg Tuck. Stretches the muscles at the back of your thighs (hamstrings) as well as the lower back.
1. Sit on the floor with your left leg straight and your right leg bent. Tuck your right foot into the groin.
2. Bend from the waist, reach forward, and clasp your left ankle. Pull your chest toward your left knee. Hold.
3. Repeat with the right leg.

Sitting Stretch. Benefits the muscles of the lower back and those behind the thighs (hamstrings).
1. Sit on the floor with your legs extended.
2. Bend slowly at the waist and bring your head toward the knees as close as possible. Keep your legs extended and your head down. Try to touch your toes and hold. This stretch should be done slowly.

Standing Straddle. Stretches the back of your thighs (hamstrings) and lower back.
1. Stand with your legs about twice shoulder width apart.
2. Place your hands on the left thigh and walk your fingers down as far as possible.
3. Bend from the waist and look forward. Hold.
4. Repeat for the right leg.

Knee Raise.

Single-Leg Tuck.

Side Stretch.

Sitting Stretch.

Standing Straddle.

LOWER THIRD

Calf Stretch. Stretches the calf muscles as well as the Achilles tendons.
1. Stand with your right leg forward and your left leg back. Keep your left leg straight and bend the right leg. Keep both feet pointed straight ahead.
2. Lean forward, keeping the heel of your left foot on the ground. Hold.
3. Repeat with the right leg.

Calf Stretch and Achilles Stretch.
1. This exercise is the same as the Calf Stretch except that you should slowly raise the heel of the rear leg as you bend the knee of the rear leg. Hold.
2. Repeat with the other leg.

Crossed-Leg Hamstring Stretch. Stretches the hamstring muscles.
1. Sit on the floor with one leg straight. Cross the other leg over the top of the straight leg. This helps stabilize the leg and prevents you from bending it during the stretch.
2. Place both hands on the straight leg and, bending slowly from the waist, walk your fingers down the leg as far as possible and hold.
3. Repeat for the other leg.

Quadricep Stretch on Side. Stretches the muscles at the front of your thighs (quadriceps).
1. Lie on your left side. Hold your right ankle with your right hand. Keep both your knees together.
2. Slowly pull the right thigh back. Do not just pull on the foot; think of moving the entire thigh. Hold.
3. Repeat for the left thigh.

Single-Leg Raise. Improves the flexibility of the muscles at the back of your thighs.
1. Lie on your back with knees bent and hands by your sides.
2. Bring the right knee toward the chest, then push the right heel toward the ceiling. Keep the left leg bent.
3. Straighten your right leg and pull your toes toward the floor.
4. Hold and repeat for the left leg.

Note: A 90-degree angle between your straight legs and hips is desirable.

Calf Stretch.

Calf Stretch and Achilles Stretch.

Crossed-Leg Hamstring Stretch.

Quadricep Stretch on Side.

Single-Leg Raise.

Sitting Ankle Rotations. Stretches the tendons and ligaments surrounding the ankles.

1. Sit on the floor; raise one foot and support it with one arm at the calf and the other hand at the foot.
2. Slowly rotate your ankle clockwise and then counterclockwise through a complete range of motion.
3. Repeat several times in each direction for each foot.

Sitting Groin Stretch. Stretches the muscles of your inner thighs (groin) and lower back.

1. Sit on the floor and place your heels together.
2. Grasp your ankles and pull your feet in toward the groin.
3. Push your knees toward the floor using your elbows.
4. Hold; straighten legs and repeat.

Sprinter.

1. Assume a squatting position with hands on the floor.
2. Extend right leg backward as far as possible. The left leg should be bent at the knee and kept under your chest. Hold.
3. Then repeat with left leg back and right leg forward.

Sprinter Start. Stretches the groin and inner muscles of your thighs (a), the groin and front of the thighs (b), and the groin and front of the ankles (c).

1. Stand with your right leg forward and bend it as you lean forward, sliding your left leg back as far as possible. Keep the left leg straight.
2. Place both hands on the floor on each side of the right foot for support.
3. Point toes (a) out to the side and hold; (b) straight ahead and hold; (c) inward and hold.
4. Repeat for the right leg.

Sitting Ankle Rotation.

Sitting Groin Stretch.

Sprinter.

Sprinter Start.   (a)   (b)   (c)

7

TRAINING FOR SPORTS

VERY FEW GOOD professional or amateur athletes play their sport to get into shape. Instead, they get into shape to play (and enjoy) their sport. Football players run, do calisthenics, and lift weights. The same is true of basketball and baseball players. Tennis players and other racquet sport enthusiasts know that by developing and maintaining a good cardiovascular system and muscle fitness they will have great staying power in the third set. For most athletes (professional and otherwise), training with free weights must be integrated into a year-long training season.

Many injuries are caused by a lack of good muscle fitness. Many fourth-quarter or last-second losses are caused by poor fitness. Many careers are shortened because of sporadic training. And, unfortunately, there are still many die-hards who believe that "natural" training is best. To this day, you hear sports buffs say that swimmers shouldn't lift weights; neither should basketball players or boxers. Wrong! All athletes can benefit from improved muscle fitness, including skeet shooters, frisbee throwers, and sailors.

Training with free weights will help you improve your performance no matter what your favorite game is. Just remember the following principles.

Principle 1. If body size (weight) is an advantage in your sport (as in football), then follow a strict training or bodybuilding regimen in the off-season for at least six months.

Principle 2. Do *not* do heavy strength and/or power training during your season if your sport requires a great deal of hand–eye coordination, as with basketball.

Principle 3. Do *not* lift heavy weights within 36 hours of a crucial sporting event.

Principle 4. Emphasize power training for better sport performance.

Principle 5. Follow a year-long plan of weight training. Here is a suggestion:

- Off-season—strength or power training.
- Two to three months before start of season—power training.
- Season—maintenance, muscle endurance on occasion, power training (once a week) if athletic events are one week apart.

Note on Principle 5: If you don't have a particular season but play all year long, or most of it, then start with power or sport training. Give yourself three to six months of serious training, but realize that your sport performance may be temporarily affected in a negative manner. After you have achieved an acceptable level of strength and power, follow Principles 1–3 above.

Principle 6. Do aerobic and/or anaerobic training as part of your overall "get into shape to play your sport" plan.

In Chapter 6, 48 exercises were provided to develop the muscles of 15 areas of your body. Following is a table designed to show which muscles need to be most conditioned to help improve your sport performance. Tennis players, for example, should strengthen the arm, shoulder, and chest muscles. Skiers will need to strengthen the hip, buttocks, thigh, and lower-leg muscles.

In order to help you improve specific muscles and muscle groups, I have included only those areas you need to emphasize. A *P* means these are primary muscles that need special attention. Two of your favorite exercises for that part of your body should be selected. An *S* means these are secondary muscles that do need conditioning, but not to the extent of the primary muscles. Here, one of your favorite exercises for that part of your body should be used. If you need to limit your lifts, stick with one primary exercise, or preferably two, and skip the secondary exercises.

Areas of the Body to be Conditioned for Improved Sports Performance

SPORTS	EXERCISES	NECK	SHOULDERS/BACK	CHEST	FRONT ARMS	BACK ARMS	FOREARMS	WAIST	ABDOMINALS	HIPS	BUTTOCKS	FRONT THIGHS	BACK THIGHS	FRONT CALVES	BACK CALVES
Archery	S	P	P	S	P	P			S			S			S
Aerobic Dancing		S							S	P	P	P	P	P	P
Backpacking		P		S					S	P		P	P	P	P
Baseball		P	S	S	P	P	P		S			P	P	S	S
Basketball		P	S				S		S	P	P	P	P	S	P
Bicycling		S							S	P		P	P	P	P
Bowling		P			S	S	P		S			S		S	S
Boxing	P	P	S			S	P	S	P	S	S	P	P	S	P
Canoeing		P	P	S	P	P			S			S		S	S
Diving	S	S	S					P	P			P	S	S	P
Fencing		P				P	P		S	P	S	P	S	S	P
Football	S	P	S			S	S	S	S	P	S	P	P	P	P
Golf		P	S		P	P	S					P			P
Gymnastics	S	P	S	S	P	P	S		P	S	S	P	S	S	P
Hockey		P	S				P		P	S	S	P	S	S	P
Lacrosse		P	S				P		S		S	P	P	P	P
Racquet Sports		P	S	S			P			S	P	P	S	S	P
Rowing		P	S	P			P		P			P	S		
Sailing		P		P			P		P			S	S	S	S
Shooting	S	P	P	S	S	P			S			S			S
Skating		P	S					S	S	P	P	P	P	P	P
Skiing				S			S		S	P	P	P	P	P	P
Soccer	S	S	S		S				S	P	P	P	P	P	P
Swimming		P	P	P	P				S			P	P	S	S
Volleyball		P	S	S				P		S	P	P	P		
Wrestling	P	P	S	P	P	P			S		S	P	S	S	P

8

PREVENTING ACHES, PAINS, AND OUCHES

IT'S DIFFICULT TO determine the number of injuries that occur in training with free weights. Most of the reported injuries focus on weightlifting—specifically injuries that occur with Olympic weightlifts. Olympic weightlifting includes the Clean and Jerk, the Snatch, and the Press. The majority of the injuries occur during the Clean and Jerk. In 1979 there were almost 11 million reported sport injuries, and 1 percent of them were caused by weightlifting. The most common injuries in weightlifting were minor sprains and strains of various muscles, ligaments, and tendons. The shoulder, low back, and knees are most susceptible to injury. Other injuries from weights include weightlifter's blackout (passing out), fracture of the bone of the forearm, and shoulder dislocation. Elevated blood pressure may be a by-product of heavy weightlifting.

Weightlifting does seem to be a relatively safe sport. Unfortunately, hard facts and figures are not available on training with free weights. In fact, there may be confusion between the terms *weightlifting* and *free weight training* when injuries are reported. It can be assumed, however, that people who train with free weights are susceptible to many of the common weightlifting injuries.

THE MOST COMMON INJURIES AND WHAT TO DO ABOUT THEM

MUSCLE SORENESS

Soreness of muscles is common during the first few weeks of many vigorous exercise programs. Training with free weights is no exception. Soreness may also occur periodically throughout your training when you try new exercises or train with heavier weights.

Muscles get sore when they are not accustomed to exercise. When muscles are called upon for extra exercise, the waste products—lactic acid and carbon dioxide—pile up in the muscle cells faster than the blood can carry them away. These surplus waste products stimulate pain receptors, which send the messages of soreness to the brain. As the muscles become more efficient, stiffness and soreness will become less noticeable and eventually disappear.

Muscle soreness can also be caused by the tearing of tiny muscle fibers during strenuous activity. This particular type of soreness may not appear at once, but usually 24–48 hours later.

To minimize the problem of sore muscles, plan your conditioning program to progress slowly and gradually, especially during the early stages. Take rest periods when you feel you need them.

Muscle soreness can be alleviated by extending the length of time devoted to warming up and tapering off. After cooling off, gently contract and relax any muscles a few times. If soreness is severe, apply ice packs to slow down the blood flow and help to prevent any possible internal bleeding or muscle hemorrhage.

STRAINS AND SPRAINS

Strains and *sprains* are often confused with each other. A strain is a tear or a pull of a muscle and/or tendon. A sprain is a tear or a stretching of a ligament.

There are three grades of muscle strain. Grade 1 strain is a srretching of a few muscle fibers. There is very little tearing. Grade 2 strain is a partial tear of the muscle fibers. Usually 10–50 percent of the fibers are involved. An experienced physician or therapist can usually feel the strain. Grade 3 strain is an extensive tear or a complete rupture of the muscle. Fifty percent, or more, of the muscle is torn. A grade 3 strain is marked by a large depression in the muscle and the inability to contract, or great difficulty in contracting, the muscle.

There are also three grades of sprain. Grade 1 sprain is a stretch of a ligament with no tear to about a 20-percent tear of the ligament. Grade 2 sprain is a moderate tear of the ligament. That is, 20–75 percent of the ligament is torn. Grade 3 sprain is a severe tear. Seventy-five percent, or more, of the ligament is torn.

The location and size of the muscle or ligament, along with the grade of the injury, will dictate how long your lifting time will be affected.

The first-aid treatment for a sprain or strain is the same— RICE, which stands for Rest, Ice, Compression, and Elevation.

The rest means using a sling, crutches, or something else to prevent the muscles or ligaments from moving while healing. Continued use or exercise could extend the injury. Ice is to be placed directly on the injury during the first 24–72 hours. Ice decreases the bleeding of the injured blood vessels by causing them to contract. Compression means placing pressure on the injured area to limit swelling. Elevation—holding the injured part of the body higher than normal—uses the force of gravity to help drain excess fluid.

The faster you apply the RICE technique, the better. Don't wait for a doctor or nurse. Place a towel over the injury. Place ice or an ice pack over the towel, covering the injured area. Then wrap an elastic bandage over the ice. *Do not wrap too tightly.* Keep on for 30 minutes. Then allow the skin to rewarm and the blood to recirculate for 15–20 minutes. Reapply. Repeat this procedure for two to three hours. If the area continues to swell, see a physician.

Follow the RICE procedure for 24–48 hours. If swelling persists 48–72 hours later, apply heat.

Further treatment will depend upon the physician, severity of the injury, and whether it is a sprain or a strain.

LOW-BACK PAIN

Lower back pain most often results from improper lifting or from trying to lift objects that are too heavy. It is common among people who bend from the waist instead of at the knees in order to lift a weight from the floor. Other reasons include improper warm-up, lack of skill, lack of adequate muscle development.

Never let the lower back arch when you are lifting weights (or any heavy object) and never bend over stiff-legged to lift. Your back can't handle this kind of stress. Always use the proper weight-lifting technique for the exercise and consciously use your leg muscles rather than your back muscles.

Many doctors believe that the onset of relatively mild lower back pain is a sign that you should become more active. Adequate regular exercise of the muscles of the abdomen will strengthen these muscles for the jobs that they have to do (such as keeping you erect and holding the organs of the abdomen in place) and will improve their tone and balance. Exercises to stretch the lower back are also important. Such exercises should also help to correct faults in posture, which may aggravate lower back strain.

WEIGHTLIFTER'S SHOULDER

Weightlifter's shoulder involves a series of ailments that can plague the lifter's deltoid muscle. In its simplest form, it is one of the most common injuries associated with the lifting of weights. The deltoid muscle—the muscle that sits like a cap over your shoulder—is the one that is usually hurt. This injury usually occurs when someone attempts to lift too much weight or performs a lift awkwardly or incorrectly. As with sprains and strains, the shoulder muscle should be treated with ice packs several times a day for two or three days. Furthermore, shoulder exercises should not be undertaken for a week or longer. If the deltoid muscles swell and become very tender, a doctor may need to be consulted. Also consider examining your technique of lifting the weight. Many times an inefficient technique contributes to this ailment.

When you return to shoulder exercises after shoulder strain injury, lift only half (or perhaps even less) of the weight you were attempting when you were injured. Stay with lighter weights, adding 2½ pounds every second to fourth session until you feel confident that your shoulder is strong enough and free from strain.

WEIGHTLIFTER'S BLACKOUT

Weightlifter's blackout is a well-recognized syndrome that is usually related to a decrease in cardiac output (the amount of blood pumped with each beat) or an irregular beat of the heart, often called *arrhythmia*. This is a particularly dangerous situation for the weight trainer since the weight can be dropped during the lifter's temporary loss of consciousness.

Many lifters or trainers experience dizziness, which may also be a warning sign of weightlifter's blackout.

While the dizziness or even the blackout is not an injury in itself, it is a very important symptom. It is usually a warning signal from your body of an impending and possibly serious condition. If you become dizzy while training (or performing any other exercise, for that matter), stop exercising immediately. Try to breathe normally but deeply. Weightlifter's blackout may be related to high blood pressure. People who train with exceptionally high weights have been reported to have blood pressures in excess of 400 mm Hg (systolic) and 300 mm Hg (diastolic). The high blood pressure may occur because of improper breathing.

Douglas McKeag, M.D., a team physician at Michigan State University and professor of family practice at the Michigan State University Medical School, says that many people do the Valsalva maneuver when lifting or training with weights. When that happens, momentary hypertension can occur. If no one is there to teach young lifters or trainers, they may hold their breath and eventually keep going for more weights. That is a bad habit. McKeag notes that, in the 1977–78 football season, 23 of 96 Michigan State University football players who trained with weights developed sustained high blood pressure. When the athletes learned how to breathe properly, decreased the emphasis on bulk, and increased the number of repetitions, only 2 of the 23 athletes remained hypertensive.

HEADACHES

Some weightlifters report headaches while lifting weights. Generally, that is due to elevated blood pressure or, again, holding the breath while lifting. Holding your breath, as indicated earlier, creates a tremendous increase in blood pressure, which may cause a temporary elevation in blood pressure.

INJURY PREVENTION

Good coaching can help prevent injuries in training with free weights. If a coach is not available, an alternative is to have someone watch you. Every lift should be observed carefully. Second, you should learn how to get away from a weight if you happen to drop it. Third, a complete stretching program should be carried out before each workout. Some of the flexibility exercises outlined in Chapter 6 are best. Fourth, you should never try to lift with your low back or do full squats. Fifth, avoid hyperextension of the back. Sixth, you should never do a maximum number of lifts without a safety rack or spotters.

In addition to these six points, proper breathing is important. The description provided in Chapter 4 gives the best technique for breathing. Just remember the following: Do not hyperventilate (breathe rapidly) before the lift. Avoid holding your breath for very long. Blackouts are caused by breath-holding followed by breathing, which causes the blood in the brain to drain into the chest cavity. The big danger here is that the lifter may collapse and be trapped or seriously injured by the bar.

9

WHERE TO BUY FREE WEIGHTS

THERE ARE NUMEROUS companies from which you may wish to purchase additional free weight equipment: benches, gloves, iron boots, plates, bars, sleeves, etc. The list in this chapter is not all-inclusive. Some of the companies may not supply all your needs, since many specialize. Also, most additional equipment can be purchased from the company or person who supplied your original free weight equipment.

Amerec Corp.
PO Box 3825
Bellevue, WA 98009

AMF-Voit, Inc.
PO Box 958
Santa Ana, CA 92702

Atlantic Fitness Products
170-A Penrod Ct.
Glen Burnie, MD 21061

Clarence Bass Ripped Enterprises
528 Chama, NE
Albuquerque, NM 87108

R. J. Bauer
2933 Ladybird Ln.
Dallas, TX 75220

Berry's Barbell & Equipment Co.
2995 E. Livingston Ave.
Columbus, OH 43205

Bicep Booster
PO Box 54861
Tulsa, OK 74155

Billard Barbell Co.
208 Chestnut St.
Reading, PA 19602

Body Exercise Equipment
2910 Kansas Ave.
Topeka, KS 66611

Buckeye Barbell
PO Box 90
Powell, OH 43065

Dick Burke's Mail Order Co.
PO Box 1211
Oklahoma City, OK 73101

The Caines Co.
PO Box 84
Greer, SC 29652

Frank Calta's Super Fitness
4241 E. Busch Blvd.
Tampa, FL 33617

Carolina Fitness Equipment
1215 Thomas Ave.
Charlotte, NC 28234

Champion Barbell
Manufacturing Div.
PO Box 1507
Arlington, TX 76010

Corbin-Gentry, Inc.
40 Maple St.
Somersville, CT 06072

Joe Corsi Fitness Equipment Co.
22570 Foothill Blvd.
Hayward, CA 94541

Custom Gym Equipment
PO Box 2073
Sinking Spring, PA 19608

Cybex, Div. of Lumex, Inc.
2100 Smithtown Ave.
Ronkonkoma, NY 11779

Dax Fitness Industries, Inc.
4101 W. Van Buren, Suite 2
Phoenix, AZ 85009

Decathlon Exercise Equipment Co.
1044 W. 74th St.
St. Paul, MN 55102

A. W. Diciolla, Jr., Co.
3460 W. 47th St.
Cleveland, OH 44102

Diversified Products Corp.
309 Williamson Ave., PO Box 100
Opelika, AL 36802

Doc's Sports
PO Box 490338
College Park, GA 30349-0338

Dynamics Health Equipment
Manufacturing Co., Inc.
1538 College Ave.
South Houston, TX 77587

East Coast Body Building
3 Willow Park Center
Farmingdale, NY 11735

Elmo's Exercise Equipment
9570 S. Utica
Evergreen Park, IL 60642

Exerco, Inc.
436 Manville Rd.
Pleasantville, NY 10570

1st Fitness International
2933 Oceanside Blvd.
Oceanside, CA 92054

Fitness America
1807½ Newport Blvd.
Costa Mesa, CA 92627

Fitness Factory
PO Box 1351
Edison, NJ 08818

Fitness Industries, Inc.
PO Box 39696
Phoenix, AZ 85069

Fitness & Nutrition Center, Inc.
2250 NE 163rd St.
North Miami Beach, FL 33160

Flex Gym Equipment
1100 W. Katella, #J
Orange, CA 92667

Fraco, Inc.
Rt. 1, PO Box 73-C
Middletown, IN 47356

Free Weight Systems, Inc.
835 Missoula Ave.
Butte, MT 59701

General Nutrition Corp.
418 Wood St., Nutrition Square
Pittsburgh, PA 15222

Johnny Gibson's Health
& Gym Equipment
52 N. 6th Ave.
Tucson, AZ 85701

Goliath Gym Equipment
4717 W. First St., Suite A
Santa Ana, CA 92703

Good Sports
610 S. Mathilda St.
Pittsburgh, PA 15224

Green Valley Gym Equipment
c/o Don Barnes
602 N. Poplar
Creston, IA 50801

Greenville Health Club
221 White Oak Rd.
Greenville, SC 29609

Hastings Barbell Co.
2257 Heath Rd.
Hastings, MI 49058

Heavyhands
PO Box 10362
Des Moines, IA 50306

Hoggan Health Equipment
6651 S. State St.
Salt Lake City, UT 84107

Huffy Corp.
2018 S. First St., PO Box 07493
Milwaukee, WI 53207

K & K Arm Strong
Fitness Equipment
1537 S. Delsea Dr.
Vineland, NJ 08360

Kreis Sports, Inc.
PO Box 120158
Nashville, TN 37212

Douglas James Leger
181 Exchange St.
Leominster, MA 01453

Life Style Products
1400 Stierlin Rd.
Mountain View, CA 94043

Dan Lurie Barbell Co., Inc.
219-10 S. Conduit Ave.
Springfield Gardens, NY 11413

Lyons Health & Fitness
213 N. Orange St.
Glendale, CA 91203

Mac Barbell Equipment
1601 NW Dallas
Grand Prairie, TX 75050

Magnum Exercise
Equipment, Inc.
8222 Jamestown Dr.
Austin, TX 78758

Malepak
PO Box 490145
Atlanta, GA 30349

Marcy Fitness Products
1736 Standard Ave.
Glendale, CA 91201

Joe Marino's Gym Equipment Co.
PO Box 144
Ridgewood, NJ 07451

Jim Moore's World Gym
5215 South Blvd.
Charlotte, NC 28210

Modern Weightlifting Products
1712 N. Genesee Dr.
Lansing, MI 48915

Steve Mott
4643 Moss Ct.
Columbus, OH 43214

National Sports Warehouse
6 Riverside Dr.
Baltimore, MD 21221

Natural Stuff, Inc.
165 Rt. 46
Rockaway, NJ 07866

Northeast Power & Fitness
1937 Washington Blvd.
Easton, PA 18042

Nu-Life Fitness
PO Box 290815
Ft. Lauderdale, FL 33329

Oakglade Industries
7707 Bankside Dr.
Houston, TX 77071

Olympia Health
& Exercise Products
5407 Wilshire Blvd.
Los Angeles, CA 90036

Olympic Health Equipment, Inc.
1717 W. Galbraith Rd.
Cincinnati, OH 45239

G. Pacillo Co., Inc.
PO Box 43
Buffalo, NY 14216

Paramount Fitness
Equipment Corp.
3000 S. Santa Fe Ave.
Los Angeles, CA 90058

Tom Petro's Health Emporium
808 S. Broad St.
Trenton, NJ 08611

Pitt Barbell & Healthfood Corp.
126 Penn Hills Mall
Pittsburgh, PA 15235

Polaris
5334 Banks St.
San Diego, CA 92110

Power Place Products, Inc.
124 E. States St.
West Lafayette, IN 47906

Power Plus
2707 Menefee
Artesia, MN 88210

Product Support
8969 Montrose Way
San Diego, CA 92122

Pro-Line
PO Box 39696
Phoenix, AZ 85069

Pro-Tron
840 Newport Center Dr.
Newport Beach, CA 92660

Quality Designs
1302 N. 8th St.
Superior, WI 54880

Rocky Mountain Gym
Equipment Co., Inc.
5745 Monaco St.
Commerce City, CO 80022

Roseglen Ironworks
11632 E. Roseglen
El Monte, CA 91732

Royal House
PO Box 1211
Oklahoma City, OK 73101

SAMCO
PO Box 088
North Ridgeville, OH 44039-0088

The Sharper Image
1 Maritime Plaza, Suite 745
San Francisco, CA 94111

Simmons Co.
54 Shallowford Rd.
Chattanooga, TN 37404

Sports Discount Center
PO Box 8418
San Francisco, CA 94128

Standard Gym Equipment, Inc.
675 Trabold Rd., PO Box 24853
Rochester, NY 14624

Stone Enterprises, Inc.
14 Hanover St., PO Box 2024
Hanover, MA 02339

Streamline Gym
& Fitness Equipment
430 Willow St.
East Stroudsburg, PA 18301

Strength, Inc.
432 Highland Ave.
Twin Falls, ID 83301

Suncoast Exercise Equipment
134 Lakeshore Dr., N.
Palm Harbor, FL 33563

Superior Gym Equipment
426 Upland Ave.
Iowa City, IA 52240

TDS Barbell & Gym Equipment
139 Banker St.
Brooklyn, NY 11222

Texas Imperial American, Inc.
PO Box 878
Tyler, TX 75710

T. K. Equipment
4 Franklin Ave.
Mt. Vernon, NY 10550

Universal Fitness Products
20 Terminal Dr., S.
Plainview, NY 11803

Universal Gym Equipment, Inc.
PO Box 1270
Cedar Rapids, IA 52406

Viking Barbell Co. & Health Club
334 Belleville Ave.
Belleville, NJ 07109

Wallingford Barbell Co.
176 N. Colony Rd.
Wallingford, CT 06492

Russ Warner's
Exercise Equipment Co.
1223 The Alameda
San Jose, CA 95126

Weider Health & Fitness, Inc.
21100 Erwin St.
Woodland Hills, CA 91367

World Barbell & Healthfoods
46 Morgantown St.
Uniontown, PA 15401

World of Health
1234 S. Garfield Ave.
Alhambra, CA 91801

Worldwide Gym Equipment
PO Box 39986
Phoenix, AZ 85069

York Barbell Co., Inc.
26-52 N. Ridge Ave., PO Box 1707
York, PA 17405

Free-weight equipment may also be purchased from local sporting goods stores or discount houses and the following chains:

Montgomery Ward

Sears, Roebuck and Co.

J. C. Penney

K-Mart

Herman's